D1341900

The
Motor Cycling Club

THE
MOTOR CYCLING CLUB

BRITAIN'S OLDEST SPORTING CLUB
FOR MOTOR CYCLES AND CARS

Peter Garnier

David & Charles
Newton Abbot   London

British Library Cataloguing in Publication
Garnier, Peter

  The Motor Cycling Club.
  1. Great Britain. Motor sports. Organisations.
  Motor cycling club, history
  I. Title
  796.7

ISBN 0-7153-9311-1

Printed in Great Britain
by Redwood Burn Ltd, Trowbridge
for David & Charles Publishers plc
Brunel House   Newton Abbot   Devon

Foreword

The MCC story is one that had to be told – if only because the Club's history embraces the history of motor sport – and, very nearly, of the motor vehicle itself. It is fitting that this book should be written now, while older Members with long memories are still around. And, with so many of the Club's events taking place in the Westcountry, it is proper that the writer should be a Cornishman who has been personally involved with the Club and its events – at first as a very young spectator, later as a competitor on two, three and four wheels, and as a reporter on *The Autocar*'s staff, covering the Club's events and activities. Peter Garnier, in his successful writing career first as a staff man, then as sports editor, and finally editor of *The Autocar*, as a writer of several books on motor sport, and as secretary and treasurer of the Grand Prix Drivers' Association for eight years has mixed freely with and become well known to all the great names in motor sport for many decades. Currently, in so-called 'retirement', he contributes regularly to *Classic Cars* – and the magazine of the British Racing Drivers' Club of which he is an associate member.

Yet, like so many, he has become saddened by the commercialism and often downright greed that so often go with today's professional motor sport and has been glad to return to the relaxed atmosphere of the MCC as a regular steward on the *Exeter* and *Land's End* Trials – and now as the chronicler of our history – putting back, as he says, some of a lifetime's pleasure that he has obtained from these events.

John Aley
Chairman, MCC

Contents

CHAPTER 1

Formative Years

From the year 1900, the tentative, trial-and-error, crude and experimental beginnings of the motor-cycle movement took hold, and the use of motor-cycles, instead of the horse, appealed to the youth of the day as a sport and pastime. During 1901, those bitten by the bug wrote letters to the motoring Press, emphasising the need for a club through which they could discuss their new-found sport, share experiences, pool ideas and form a motor-cyclists' brotherhood. In October 1901, therefore, an enterprising man by the name of T. Underwood called a public meeting at Frascati's Restaurant, in London. Almost thirty people turned up, and it was unanimously agreed to form a club – named, predictably, *The* Motor Cycling Club for the very good reason that there weren't any others. As a result of this historic meeting, the MCC was officially founded on 19 November 1901.

There have been differences of opinion as to whether the MCC is the oldest motor-sporting club in Britain; but, since the Midland Automobile Club was founded on 11 January 1901, ten months earlier, this claim can not be made without qualification – if at all. The two organisations exist, however – and have always existed – for two entirely different purposes, the MAC to run its famous Shelsley Walsh speed hill-climb, principally for cars, and the MCC to run long-distance reliability trials initially for motor-cycles alone, but subsequently opening their entry lists to cars as well; and, later, to run speed events for both classes on closed racing circuits – with the emphasis, though, on regularity, rather than sheer speed. Both clubs, therefore, can co-exist peacefully, each claiming with every justification to be the oldest of its kind. And, come to that, what are ten months in an elapsed time of eighty-eight years?

The first president of the Club was S. F. (Selwyn) Edge who, like his friend and rival Charles Jarrott, had been a successful racing cyclist, each turning to De Dion motor-tricycles and then, in Edge's case, to Napier cars. With one of these he was to become famous as the winner of the 1902 Gordon Bennett race (then run from Paris to Innsbruck in conjunction with the Paris-Vienna) with his cousin Cecil Edge as riding-mechanic. He was to add further glory to his name when, in 1907, he set up a 24-hour record, covering 1,582 miles single-handed in a Napier on the Brooklands track, which had opened on 17 June that year. The choice of Edge as president in those early, formative years was a wise one for the MCC; not only was he a teetotaller and immensely fit and hard-working, but he was acutely aware of the publicity value of success. Other officials were as follows:

1924: The importance with which success in MCC trials was regarded is shown by this advertisement appearing in the issue of *The Motor Cycle* reporting the London-Exeter Trial. The Collier brothers were responsible for the original Matchless motor-cycles.

Vice-Presidents: E. Kennard, JP, J. Pennell, Mark Mayhew
Captain: E. H. Arnott
Vice-Captains: F. R. Johns, M. T. Tuckman
Hon Solicitors: J. B. and F. Purchase
Hon Treasurer: E. March
Hon Secretary: G. E. Roberts
Hon Auditor: A. J. Wilson
Committee: R. G. Booth, S. H. Fry, B. A. Hunt, J. van Hooydonk, W. Kennett, E. Perman, Mervyn O'Gorman, A. G. Quibell.

For the first few months, the Committee confined themselves to social gatherings, 50-mile runs out of town, and a few minor competitions. In 1902 they began to branch out and make themselves known, with Club Captain E.H. Arnott completing the run from Land's End to John O'Groats in 65 hr 45 min on a French-built Werner motor-cycle. In April of the same year they ran their first race meeting, which – under the heading 'Motor Cycling at The Crystal Palace' – was reported with an ingenuous journalistic charm in *The Autocar* of 1 March 1902, a journal of which, many years later, I was to become sports editor and then editor. So unfamiliar is the punctuation in the list of results that I have altered it to comply with current style:

On Saturday afternoon last, taking advantage of the motor exhibition at the Palace, which closed on that day, The Motor Cycling Club held their first race meeting by arranging three races and three speed and hill-climbing contests for motor-cyles. The machines were classified under three heads, viz: (1) for motor bicycles driven by motors catalogued by the makers at $1^1/_2$hp and under. (2) machines with motors catalogued by the makers at more than $1^1/_2$hp and not exceeding 2hp. And (3) for machines fitted with motors catalogued at more than 2hp. The classification for the speed and hill-climbing events was exactly similar. The distance in each competition on the track was five miles, while the speed and hill-climbing course had its start on the road in the rear of the track, and its finish on the Grand Terrace. This event but provides speed and hill-climbing comparison only between each machine competing, as neither the length of the course nor the special or average gradients were vouchsafed to the public. The races were held under NCU rules, pedalling after the start being thereby allowable. The cement track was, thanks to the fine weather overhead, dry and in good condition, but the road course was extremely holding and heavy owing to the rapid thaw. The officials were: *Judge*, A. J. Wilson: *Timekeepers*: Harry J. Swindley, H. H. Griffin, and F. T. Bidlake.

1912:The road to Exeter was long, wet and rough – but did not seem to daunt this competitor as he set off with a cigar clenched between his teeth, the double carbide headlamps emitting a warm – if not illuminating – glow.

RESULTS

Event 1 (five miles):

First heat: 1, E. Dries (Derby motor-cycle, $1^1/_2$hp). 2, T. B. Lindre (Derby $1^1/_2$ hp). Time, 10min 36sec.

Second heat: 1, T. H. Tessier (Werner $1^1/_2$hp f.d.). 2, Bert Yates (Humber $1^1/2$hp). A. Rivett (Blizzard $1^1/_2$hp) stopped. The Werner travelled, and was driven, splendidly, doing 9min 18sec, Tessier assisting the engine by much pedalling. Yates' time was 10min 7sec.

Final Heat: 1, T. H. Tessier (Werner $1^1/_2$hp f.d.). 2, E. Dries (Derby $1^1/_2$ hp). Others stopped. Tessier won by three laps, doing 9min $29^2/_5$sec. Dries's time was 11min $12^2/_5$sec.

Event 2 (five miles): Owing to the small number of starts, this contest was run off in one heat, which resulted as follows: H. W. Stones, on the $1^3/_4$hp Rex, won anyhow in 9min 40sec, L. S. Watson on $1^3/_4$ hp Chapelle, running on to turf.

Event 3: H. Martin, on Excelsior $2^3/_4$hp, won easily in 9min $4^4/_5$sec; A. Westlake, on 3hp Chapelle, doing 9min $28^1/_5$sec, but being disqualified by reason of his starter running with him over the mark.

SPEED AND HILL-CLIMBING CONTEST

Event 1: 1, A. Rivett ($1^1/_2$ hp Blizzard), 2min $5^2/_5$sec . 2, Bert Yates ($1^1/_2$hp Humber), 2min $16^4/_5$sec. 3, E. Perman ($1^1/_2$hp Excelsior), 2min 22sec. 4, J. van Hooydonk ($1^1/_2$hp Phoenix), 2min $22^2/_5$sec. 5, T. H. Tessier ($1^1/_2$hp Werner f.d.), 2min $31^3/_5$sec. 6, L. Dillon ($1^1/_2$hp A.M.I.), 2min $38^2/_5$sec.

Event 2: 1, E. T. Arnott ($1^3/_4$hp Princeps), 2min $13^4/_5$sec. 2, H. W. Stones ($1^3/_4$hp Rex), 2min $17^4/_5$sec.

Event 3: 1, H. Martin ($2^3/_4$hp Excelsior) 2min $6^2/_5$sec.

During the next couple of years various minor trials, runs into the country and social events were organised, a period during which the ACC was founded, running its first 1,000-mile trial, the mileage spread over a fortnight in short, there-and-back runs. Legal speed limits were raised in 1903 from 12 to 20mph, with reduced limits of 5 and 10mph at certain danger points; 375 motor-cycles were exhibited at the 1903 Stanley Show; the first sidecar was marketed; and there was much controversy as to whether automatic or mechanical inlet valves were best.

Changes were made in the Club's officers. Early in 1904 the Hon Secretary resigned and was replaced by J. Horace Reeves; and Ernest Perman replaced J. Pennell as a Vice-President. The Committee was strengthened by the addition of C. W. Brown, who was appointed Trials Hon Secretary; and the Reverend B. H. Davies (later to become famous as 'Ixion' of *The Motor Cycle* magazine) undertook the editorship of the Club's *Gazette*, published monthly and printed by Temple Press. In the general picture, 1904 saw no fewer than 21,521 motor-cycles registered in Britain by mid-summer, 488 motor-cycles exported by Britain in six months, experiments with 3-inch tyres (the standard size being 28 by 2in) – and a speed of 76.5mph achieved by a lightweight motor-cycle in France.

As an illustration of the sort of speed and reliability that were becoming possible on the roads of 1904, G. P. Mills, on a Raleigh, completed the 900-odd miles between Land's End and John O'Groats in slightly under 51 hours, averaging almost 18mph in bad weather conditions that had reduced the already poor roads to a mudbath. Such a 'true' motor-cycle, without 'light pedal assistance', could pack 30-odd miles into each hour for short periods over good roads.

The year 1904 was particularly significant for the MCC, for it brought the first of the Club's long-distance 'classic' trials – 'The Motor Cycle London to Edinburgh Ride'. Conceived by Arthur Candler (who became Hon Secretary in 1905) and held at Whitsun, this event was to become famous as simply *The Edinburgh*, continuing (if only in name) to the present day as one of the MCC's three, annual 'classic' trials.

The event attracted no fewer than seventy entries, though the less ambitious Committee members had resisted such a marathon on the grounds that few, if any, would ever reach Edinburgh – and that the spluttering, fitful acetylene gas lamps would result in a succession of night-time accidents. The start was near the General Post Office, then in St Martins-le-Grand, late in the evening, with the route leading straight up the Great North Road, water-bound, stony and dusty in dry weather, with an abundance of horse-shoe nails to cause punctures, and a rutted, slippery mudbath in the wet. Only two hills were included: Alconbury, which was loose and badly rutted; and Alnwick, which was next best thing to a trials hill. There were no time controls, as there are in today's events, competitors having enough to contend with already – and concerned only with getting there in the twenty-four hours allowed.

In his very brief history of *The Edinburgh* (*The Autocar*, 31 August 1945), J. A. ('Jackie') Masters – of whom we shall hear a great deal more, later on – wrote the following:

Friday evening, May 20, 1904 – scene, the General Post Office in the shadow of St Paul's Cathedral. At 9.52pm, J. A. Jackson, captain of the MCC, could contain his patience no longer and (8 minutes before the official starting time) he despatched C. W. Brown, on his $2^3/_4$hp FN motor-cycle, No. 1 in the first London-to-Edinburgh club run, to the cheers of a very large crowd of onlookers of which the writer (with his $2^1/_4$hp Jehu) was one.

The proceedings had opened with what the official record describes as a 'generous supper' at Huggetts Hotel, Paternoster Square, with S. F. Edge in the chair, supported by other motoring notabilities, including D. Napier, Mervyn O'Gorman and Lt-Col Mark Mayhew. Out of an entry of 70, 46 actual starters were present and the aforementioned official record goes on to say that, having been fed, they filed past the president to the strains of *'Ave Selwyn, hi morituri te salutant'*.

The last man having been despatched, the officials made a dash for the 11.38pm from King's Cross to Grantham in a couple of overcrowded hansoms. S. H. Fry was extremely peeved because, having to sit on the footboard in the pouring rain, his *silk hat* had been ruined!

Despite the Committee's fears, of the 70 entries, a total of 46 started, 34 of them completing the 400 miles within the time limit; of the 15 motor-tricycles that started, 4 finished. This event, and those that followed, provided a first class proving ground in which accessory and component manufacturers could try out their products. Among these was an electrical equipment company who entered their representative, riding an Ormonde equipped with electric lighting, the power being supplied by four 20-ampere/hour batteries in a special tin container on the luggage-grid. He was among those that finished within the 24-hour limit. Also among the competitors in this first 'Edinburgh Ride' were the brothers Lionel and Douglas Baddeley, the former becoming President in 1945. This is an early example of the strong 'brand loyalty' that has existed among MCC members throughout its eighty-eight years.

So confident of the long-distance capabilities of members' motor-cycles did the ambitious, forceful Selwyn Edge become that, in 1905, he presented a vast cup to be awarded to the winner of a non-stop run. The organising committee, acutely doubtful (as ever) of Edge's optimism, laid out a short, 20-mile circuit in Hertfordshire, confident that the Cup would be won or lost (hopefully, the latter) after two or three brief laps on a Saturday afternoon. Instead, although most competitors retired quickly, Jones on a home-made 'special' and Milligan on a 3hp Bradbury continued to lap the circuit interminably – to the satisfaction of Edge, and the deep concern of the organisers, who began to doubt their ability to maintain the supply of observers. It was not until well into the night that, to their relief, Milligan retired and Jones – still lapping happily – won the Cup. History does not record whether he was allowed to continue until he, too, retired – or was shown the chequered flag immediately.

1909: Warmly dressed for the occasion, a group of competitors takes part in an MCC Club Run – young men who, only ten or so years before, would have been enjoying their sport on four legs, rather than two wheels.

The annual London-Edinburgh, with its traditional Whitsun date, quickly grew in stature to become a much-publicised national event. In 1905, when there were no fewer than 28,000 motor-cycles registered on the roads of Britain, there were 88 entries. Of these, 59 started and 22 finished within the 24 hours' allowance to receive Gold Medals. The route ran through Biggleswade, Grantham, Wetherby, Durham, Alnwick, Berwick-on-Tweed and Levenhall – whence enthusiastic members of the Edinburgh Motoring Club escorted competitors along the remaining seven miles to the finish.

It was decided in 1906 that the Club's increasing activities warranted a Trials Secretary, and J. van Hooydonk was appointed, a name that was to become well known in the MCC through the years, both as a competitor and official. The London-Edinburgh Ride became officially The London to Edinburgh and Back, with a time limit of 48 hours for the double journey; the 'and Back' was optional (as it had, in fact, been in previous 'Edinburghs', though nobody seems to have completed the double journey). And, for the first time in an MCC trial, cars were admitted, provided they cost £250 or less, which virtually limited the car entry to light cars and cyclecars. Seventeen cars left the start – six Rovers, three De Dions, a Humber, New Orleans, Maxwell, Pope Tribune, Crypto, Belsize, Panhard and Peugeot.

Until the Club's formation in 1901, the viable motor-cycles (as distinct from tricycles) had been a rarity, so that the MCC and the breed virtually grew up together. So far as cars were concerned, when the Club first admitted motorists in 1906, things were very different, and at this stage it is interesting to look briefly at the motoring scene. The first practicable cars had been produced in Germany by Karl Benz and Gottlieb Daimler as far back as 1885–6, with confirmation in contemporary news-cuttings still available today. Despite this, however, national claims are at variance.

The Motor of 29 September 1936 (p.360) states: 'In a little more than a month from now we shall be celebrating in this country the fortieth anniversary of the beginning of motoring here' – by which one assumes they meant the passing of the Motor Car Act in November 1896. And, in his Foreword to his *The Antique Automobile*, the late St John Nixon refers to '. . .the British Motor Industry, which will be celebrating its Diamond Jubilee in November 1956' – its sixtieth year, in fact, which ties up with *The Motor's* statement 20 years before. Yet it was in 1985 that the British Motor Industry celebrated the 100th Anniversary of the Automobile – eighty-nine years after the Motor Car Act. Daimler-Benz, however, with every justification as builders of the first viable motor-cars in 1886, held their 'Mercedes-Benz Historical' in August 1986. By way of light relief, and not to be taken too seriously, an American by the name of George B. Selden announced in 1899 that he was the inventor of the automobile!

Whatever the claims, there is no doubt that, by the *Edinburgh* of 1906, when cars were first admitted to the events, the motor car had been developing steadily and quickly for some twenty years, and had reached a relatively advanced state. There had been the heroic, town-to-town events, with the 1895 Paris-Bordeaux-Paris, for example, and the 1896 Paris-Marseilles-Paris respectively covering 732 and 1,062 miles. These though, had been terminated abruptly with the disastrous Paris-Madrid of 1903, halted at Bordeaux after a succession of fatal accidents – with Gabriel's Mors in front, having averaged more than 60mph on unguarded, unclosed public roads, thronged along the route by thousands of unprotected spectators. Charles Jarrott, the MCC's President from 1908 to 1922, had been a competitor in this race, leading the French De Dietrich team – and the field – as No. 1.

There had been the six Gordon Bennett races (1900–05), leading to the first Grand Prix of the Automobile Club de France in 1906, run over a distance of 390 miles, compared with today's 200-mile 'sprints', and won by Szisz' Renault at 66.8mph. And there had been Tourist Trophy races, Targa Florios and the rest. High speeds over immense distances were nothing new to the big racing cars by 1906 – but for the delicate little light cars and cyclecars of the day, London to Edinburgh and, possibly, back was formidable.

By now the MCC had settled upon the basic style of event that was to become familiar to competitors in this and their other 'classic' trials through to the present day. Instead of competing against each other, as in a race, they competed against the Club. Thus, if everyone completed the journey to schedule, unpenalised for arriving late or early at controls, or for passing 'secret checks', before or after the stipulated time-limits, or for 'footing' or stopping on any of the 'observed sections' (which meant trials hills of increasing severity as the years went by), then everyone could win a Premier Award – a Gold Medal. Failure to comply with just one of these requirements resulted in a Second Class Award (a Silver); and two failures produced a Third (Bronze). More than two, and you got (and still get) nothing. These awards, hallmarked in the case of the Gold and Silver, were discontinued in 1931 on the grounds of economy, though their original designations still linger on among older members.

Thus, with the emphasis on regularity and reliability, as distinct from speed, together with observed performances on special sections, clear of public roads, these events became, and still are, acceptable to the authorities and the police. And Club officials – then as now – visited and appeased residents in country districts where a concentration of competing vehicles might inconvenience local residents. It is for these reasons that the MCC trials have survived through 87-odd years, unaffected by the controversy that surrounds rallies.

The following year, 1907, was an important one for the Club. It was agreed at the January committee meeting that application should be made for affiliation to the Auto Cycle Club (soon to become the Auto Cycle Union, governing body of motor cycle sport in the UK) – at an annual fee of 2/- (10p) per MCC member, which included the ACC's magazine. Previously there had been a degree of antagonism between the two organisations, the MCC as a democratic, enterprising body running an extensive yearly programme of social and sporting events, in which the great majority of members competed. The ACC, in contrast, was composed of nominated and slightly ingenuous members – initially, at least – whom the MCC felt were lacking in first-hand experience of the sport they sought to represent.

The dynamic Selwyn Edge was replaced as President by Major Sir H. E. Colville, and the 1907 fixture list included twelve sporting events of various types. The there-and-back *Edinburgh*, with its 10/6 (57$^1/_2$p) entry fee for motor-cycles and £1.1s (105 pence) for cars competing for the Schulte Cup, and the maximum cost price for car entries raised to £550, seemed to have become almost easy. No fewer than 36 motor-cycles (out of 62 entries), 4 tri-car and sidecar outfits (10) and 12 cars (18) qualified for Gold Medals, having completed the run to Edinburgh inside the twenty-four hours' allowance. Among the successful motor-cyclists was W. O. Bentley on a twin-cylinder Quadrant, whose cars were later to become world-famous; and C. A. Vandervell (founder of the world-famous bearing manufacturers, Vandervell Products, and driving force behind the Vanwall G. P. cars) won a 'Gold' in the car class, driving a 17-21hp Daimler.

A special Gold Medal, awarded by the ACC to affiliated clubs, was won by S. G. Frost (4$^1/_2$hp Minerva twin) for the best there-and-back performance on a motor-cycle; and the Schulte Cup for a similar performance by a car went to J. Platt-Betts (8hp Rover) – eight riders/drivers being awarded 'Golds' by the MCC, for the there-and-back, double run. A Miss A. M. Hind, driving a 24hp Deasy car (No. 80) – with 'Magneto and Accumulators ignition' – appears in the programme for this event. She may be the first-ever woman competitor in an MCC trial, and she qualified for a Gold Medal for the single, London-Edinburgh section.

Bentley and Vandervell were not the only members whose names were to become household words in the motor-cycle and motor industries in later years. There was William Morris, later Lord Nuffield; and Victor Riley, who won a 'Gold' in a speed hill-climb run by the MCC in April 1907 on Sharpenhoe Hill, a stretch of public road five miles to the north of

1908: One of the few photographic records surviving from the very early days, this shot is of the Club's Chairman, R. H. Heard, taken at Stoney Cross during the London-to-Land's End.

Luton. In the same event, W. Gunn tied for fastest time of the day with O. P. C. Collier, later a famous name in the motor-cycle industry. It was a case of 'win a little, lose a little', though, for the resignation of T. Sopwith was accepted in February 1907. These and many other founder members of the British motor and motor-cycle industries featured regularly in those early entry-lists – understandably enough, as they made a start up the ladder of the great industries they were later to create and serve. Another name that appears regularly in the entry-lists and in minutes of committee meetings was Head – later to collaborate as 'Caput' in *The Autocar's* column 'The Sport' with the great 'Sammy' Davis, who also was to compete in MCC trials from the early days through to the end of the 1930s.

Club membership stood at 200 by April 1907 – with, as the Hon Treasurer reported, cash-in-hand totalling £107 5s 9d of which £20 was paid to the ACC for affiliation at 2/- per head of membership. Further taxing their resources, the Club was fined for failing to display a 'Registered Office' plate outside their premises – the Tudor Hotel in London's Oxford Street. This meeting place was moved in November 1908 to Pagani's Restaurant, 44 Great Portland Street, where meetings were held through to March 1940, when World War II put a temporary end to activities.

A revealing discussion was held at the July 1907 committee meeting regarding the scanty coverage of Club events in the RAC's *Journal* and other 'Motoring Papers'. Instead of sending staff men to cover such events, it seems that journals relied upon reports submitted by the Club itself – and that the blame lay with the committee for sending them in too late! There was no shortage of events to be covered for, apart from the *Edinburgh*, already well established were the opening run to Brighton, Easter Tour, 200 miles Reliability Trial, 100 miles Passenger Trial, Inter-Team Trial, Petrol Consumption Trial, and a host of social events. In 1907 alone, 71 'Golds', 26 'Silvers' and 14 'Bronzes' were awarded to competitors in these events.

Upon the death of Sir H. E. Colville, it was agreed to invite Sir Arthur Conan Doyle to take over as President in 1908 – with, as a sort of 'second best', an invitation to Charles Jarrott in case Sir Arthur was unable to accept. It was fortunate, perhaps, that he declined, Jarrott being the better bet so far as the Club was concerned. He was an old friend and rival of Selwyn Edge from the days when they first raced motor-tricycles together, subsequently becoming well known as a racing driver, a gifted motoring historian, and one of the foremost campaigners in the motoring movement. He was a founder member of the Society of Motor Manufacturers and Traders, and had abandoned a successful legal career to devote himself to the cause of motoring, for which he saw a brilliant future as the greatest single innovation ever devised by man.

He was to remain as President until 1922.

One of Jarrott's first moves as President was to introduce the 600-mile London-to-Land's End and Back 'run' to the Club's already formidable list of sporting events for 1908, presenting the principal trophy, the Jarrott Cup. Because of the shortage of time to get the event organised, the route chosen, and to woo the co-operation of local residents, the dates were fixed for 3 and 4 August, instead of the Easter holiday weekend which was later to become the traditional date for the event. For this first-ever *Land's End*, the entry was limited to motor-cycles, tri-cars and sidecar outfits. Fifteen hours each were allowed for the 300-mile outward and return journeys, with an hour's rest-halt at Exeter on each.

The entry fee was one guinea, and competitors were sent off in pairs from the Berkeley Arms, Cranford Bridge (12 miles to the west of London), the first pair leaving at 4am on August Bank Holiday. Only twenty-six entries were received – presumably because the ACU were holding their London-Plymouth-London, 24-hour run at the same time. The ever-successful S. G. Frost won the Jarrott Cup, with a total error of 3min 36sec, to Summers' 4min 3sec in second place. Only eight finished the double-journey, two with 'Golds' and six with 'Silvers'.

Today, when one can knock-off the journey from London to Land's End in a comfortable $5^1/_2$ hours, the significance of this event to people in the far south-west is difficult to imagine. Crowds lined the narrow, twisting dirt-roads, cheering-on the muddy, dusty, travel-stained competitors, profoundly impressed by their achievement. London was infinitely far-off, almost another world. For the local people then, and for many years to come, Truro was their Mecca. That the competitors were going to turn round and ride back to London seemed beyond belief. Their achievement was the more impressive because, only a couple of years before, the *Daily Mail* had published an article headed 'The Failure of the Motor-Cycle' in which they had described the machine as 'The Cinderella of the wheel trade'.

The *Edinburgh* was held on its usual Whitsun Bank Holiday dates, with 133 motor-cycle entries, 7 tri-cars and side-cars, and 28 cars. The enterprising Muriel Hind, having won a 'Gold' the previous year in her Deasy car, took to two wheels for this event, riding a Rex – and completing the London-Edinburgh section in twenty-two hours to win another 'Gold'. As well as the hardy annuals such as W. O. Bentley, C. A. Vandervell, Victor Riley and others, the entry included George Brough (Brough), later to become well known for his Brough Superior motor-cycles, and – much later – cars; and for his checked caps. There was also Captain Sir R. K. Arbuthnot, Royal Navy (see appendix 3), who continued to compete on two wheels in this and other

MCC trials after being promoted Rear-Admiral!

Because it was felt that car drivers were receiving preferential treatment with their Schulte Cup, a special MCC Challenge Cup was introduced for the motor-cycle entries, the winner being S. G. Frost on a $4^1/_2$hp, twin-cylinder Minerva. Platt-Betts again won the Schulte Cup with his 8hp Rover, becoming the holder *in perpetuo*. Of the 168 entries, 67 won 'Golds', and 2 'Silvers'. Double-journey 'Golds' were won by 14 competitors, including Miss A. E. Woods with an 8hp Rover car.

For the first time, it appears, a few competitors fell foul of the Law for speeding – or 'scorching' as they probably called it then. Among several others, C. H. Crole-Rees was fined £3 2s, plus 18s costs, at the St Neots County Court. *The Motor Cycle* advised 'We understand from a victim that it is best for the offending motorists to appear at the Court in person.' To such an extent did the Club frown upon these transgressions that a letter was sent to all successful competitors asking if any police complaints had been made against them. As a result, one or two awards were withheld, A. S. Phillips losing his double-journey 'Gold' through a 'Driving to the danger . . .' conviction at Retford. Rex Mundy, another who was to become famous in the industry, lost his too, as the result of a speeding conviction.

There seemed to be no holding Miss Hind. In *The Motor Cycle* of 1 July 1908, it was reported that she had abandoned her plans to make the Land's End to John O'Groats, 'end-to-end' run on her tri-car because of the difficulty in finding a woman passenger to accompany her. Undaunted therefore, she made the run unaccompanied, on a solo motor-cycle!

At this stage there were still no motor-car members as such, so that there was no problem in re-affiliating the entire membership when the ACC became the ACU. To enter a car in an MCC event one had to be a motor-cycle member – and only the entrant could drive it. The car, however, did not have to belong to the entrant.

The slightly hostile atmosphere that had existed between the MCC and ACU continued through 1908 and, at the end of the year, it was voted by 35 to 7 to discontinue affiliation in 1909. A most interesting entry exists in the Minutes Book for 1908 'tacitly agreeing' to ban speedometers on vehicles competing in the *Edinburgh*. If the number of 'Golds' won by members couldn't be whittled down by the introduction of non-stop, observed sections, the organising committee had no difficulty, apparently, in resorting to other means! Nor were the members at a loss for ideas. A competitor in a long-distance event had his 'Gold' confiscated when it was discovered that he had managed to reach a control by humping his broken-down motor-cycle on to a horse-drawn cart.

CHAPTER 2

Gaining Impetus

Having run their first race-meeting for motor-cycles at the Crystal Palace in 1902 (thought to be the first motor-cycles-only race meeting ever run in this country), the Club was anxious to continue running racing events. The new Brooklands track (see Chapter 9), where motor-cycles had first raced on 18 April 1908, was an obvious choice – and it was another major decision taken during Jarrott's first year in office as President to add a Brooklands meeting to the list of annual events. Approaches were made to the Brooklands Automobile Racing Club (the 'Brooklands' becoming 'British' in January 1949 after the demise of the track), and the Outer Circuit was booked (at a fee of £25) for 16 October 1909. Thereby came about the third of the Club's annual 'classics', joining the *Edinburgh* and *Land's End*.

The meeting was open to non-members as well as members, the machines taking part being either out-and-out racers or road versions stripped and tuned for racing, and the meeting continued in this form for many years. Gradually though, it was felt that these regulations were unsatisfactory as they precluded members' ordinary road machines – the very type for which the Club had sought to cater from its earliest days. It was not until 1925, though (with a break from 1914 for WWI), that the rules were changed, and the One-Hour High-Speed Trials (with a set minimum distance for each engine capacity class), and the flat-out flying lap were introduced – respectively nicknamed 'The One-Hour Blind' and 'The Dash'.

In 1911 the *Motor Cycle* Championship was introduced at this meeting,

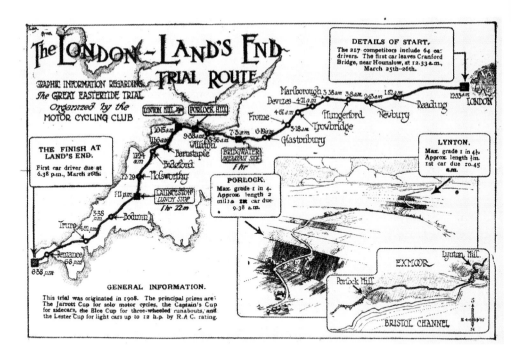

The LONDON—LAND'S END TRIAL ROUTE

GRAPHIC INFORMATION REGARDING
The GREAT EASTERTIDE TRIAL
Organized by the
MOTOR CYCLING CLUB

LYNTON HILL · PORLOCK HILL

DETAILS OF START.
The 217 competitors include 64 car drivers. The first car leaves Cranford Bridge, near Hounslow, at 12.33 a.m., March 25th—26th.

THE FINISH AT LAND'S END.
First car due at 6.38 p.m., March 26th.

LYNTON.
Max. grade 1 in 4½.
Approx. length ½m.
1st car due 10.45 a.m.

PORLOCK.
Max grade 1 in 4.
Approx. length 2 miles. 1st car due 9.38 a.m.

BRIDGWATER BREAKFAST STOP.
1 hr

LAUNCESTON LUNCH STOP.
1 hr 22 m

Marlborough 3.38 a.m. · 3.8 a.m. · 2.43 a.m. · 1.52 a.m. · Reading · 12.33 a.m. LONDON
Devizes 4.21 a.m. · Hungerford · Newbury
Frome 4.51 a.m. · Trowbridge 5.18 a.m.
Glastonbury 6.8 a.m. · 5.57 a.m.
Williton 9.8 a.m. · 8.56 a.m. · 7.3 a.m.
10.45 a.m. · 11.6 a.m. · Barnstaple · Bideford · 11.54 a.m.
Holsworthy 12.29
Bodmin 3.38 p.m. · 5.11 p.m.
Truro 4.51 p.m.
Penzance 6.8 p.m.
6.38 p.m.

EXMOOR · Lynton Hill · Porlock Hill
BRISTOL CHANNEL

GENERAL INFORMATION.
This trial was originated in 1908. The principal prizes are: The Jarrott Cup for solo motor cycles, the Captain's Cup for sidecars, the Elce Cup for three-wheeled runabouts, and the Lester Cup for light cars up to 12 h.p. by R.A.C. rating.

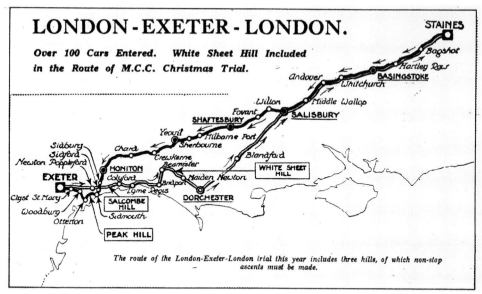

LONDON - EXETER - LONDON.

Over 100 Cars Entered.   White Sheet Hill Included in the Route of M.C.C. Christmas Trial.

STAINES
Bagshot
Hartley Row
BASINGSTOKE
Andover · Whitchurch
Middle Wallop
Wilton · SALISBURY
Fovant
SHAFTESBURY
Yeovil · Tilborne Port
Sherborne
Chard · Crewkerne · Beaminster · Blandford
Sidbury · WHITE SHEET HILL
Sidford
Newton Poppleford · HONITON
EXETER · Colyford
Clyst St. Mary · Lyme Regis · Bridport · Maiden Newton
Woodbury · SALCOMBE HILL · DORCHESTER
Otterton · Sidmouth
PEAK HILL

The route of the London-Exeter-London trial this year includes three hills, of which non-stop ascents must be made.

In the twenties and thirties *The Autocar*, *The Motor Cycle* and their contemporaries would devote four or five pages to reports of MCC trials; and two or three to previews, giving details of the route, interesting hills, and entries (even to their registration numbers!). These maps are from issues of *The Autocar* in 1921 and 1922, and are typical of the beautifully prepared route maps.

the winner being awarded the valuable Harry Smith Gold Challenge Cup, a trophy that has had an intriguing history. After being awarded annually at this Brooklands meeting through the years, it was lodged for safe-keeping during World War II at a jeweller's in The Strand, London, where it was badly damaged during the bombing and went missing. A scarcely recognisable, battered – though gold – cup was eventually recovered and restored at the insurers' expense, all traces of engraving being obliterated in the process. Is today's 'MCC Gold Cup' (awarded for the best performance by a production motor-cycle up to 1,000cc at the annual Silverstone meetings) the original Harry Smith cup, as believed – or is it some entirely extraneous, though important, trophy with its origins lost for ever? And a proportion of its gold, too?

The year 1909 was significant in many ways in the field of motor-cycle sport. The regulations for the Isle of Man Tourist Trophy races, first held in 1907, were re-framed free of a fuel consumption formula. The Scottish Six Days' Trial was inaugurated; and the British Motor Cycle Racing Club was founded. Less 'sporting' by far, the Road Board and Road Fund were introduced by Parliament, the latter to raise funds for the upkeep of the roads. Though unpopular, it was understandable – though not so the uses to which this Fund is put today!

A design by Club member H. Karslake for a 'handlebar badge' was submitted at the 15 April 1909 committee meeting and approved – very much on the lines of the now familiar MCC badge, with its 'sprocket' border surrounding a single-cylinder De Dion motor-cycle engine on a blue background.

The following month an extremely handsome cup was presented to the Club by the Rover Company, one of the pioneers in the British motor industry, whose origins extended back to 1877, when J. K. Starley (later to become an active MCC member) and W. Sutton began making penny-farthings and tricycles, using the trade-name 'Rover' for one of their products. In 1896, Starley and Sutton had become the Rover Cycle Company, entering the motor-cycle industry with a $2^{1}/_{2}$hp Rover in 1903. The first of their four-wheelers had been the 8hp single-cylinder, in which Platt-Betts, Miss Woods and others had distinguished themselves in MCC events – and in one of which Dr J. K. Jefferson had driven from London to Constantinople (Istanbul) in 1906. A smaller, 6hp 'single' followed the 8hp in 1906, selling at £105. It was a very appropriate decision, therefore, that the Rover Challenge Cup should be awarded for the best two-way run in the London-Edinburgh-London by a light car with catalogue value not exceeding £250, without accessories.

In the ensuing *Edinburgh*, the Rover Cup (which, in the intervening two or three weeks, had been stolen from the Rover showroom and replaced by the insurance company) was won by R. O. Clarke, driving a 10/12hp FN, with D. H. Whitehead second (7hp Anser) and A. Meschini third in an 8hp Rover. Of the 134 starters, 44 solo motor-cycles, 7 passenger machines and 14 cars won 'Golds'. For the double run, 16 solos, 1 passenger machine and 5 cars (including Miss Hind, this time in her Deasy) won 'Golds' – a remarkable performance in view of the ban on speedometers, the state of the roads and the indifferent signposting – although the AA 'Guide' and their yellow-enamelled circular 'Village Signs' (showing the distances to the nearest hamlet, in both directions) had been around since the previous year. Among other things, this Handbook listed in some seventy pages, 1,500 AA Road agents, given under counties, and in alphabetical order of towns and villages. From them, the traveller could find what sort of service to expect, and the tyres stocked – 'Cl (Clincher), Cli (Clipper), Des (Desclee), J (Jenatzy), S (Sirdar)', and so on.

A red-letter day in the history of the Club – in more senses than one – occurred in July 1909, when the Hon Secretary was authorised to buy himself a typewriting machine. He put it into immediate use, typing the Minutes of monthly committee meetings alternately in black and red. Until then, the Minutes had been written laboriously, and often illegibly, by hand.

Eighteen teams took part in the 1909 Inter-Team Trial – the MCC themselves taking first place from the often successful Coventry and Warwickshire Motor Cycle Club – and thereby becoming winners of the first competition for the *Motor Cycle* Challenge Cup. The price of gold seems to have been pretty reasonable in those days, and nepotism rife, for all members of the winning team were unanimously voted to receive Gold Medals.

For the 1909 Jarrott Cup, alias the London-Land's End-London, held again over the August Bank Holiday, the entry fee was set at 10s 6d ($52^1/_2$p), and the ban on speedometers was lifted – presumably owing to its negligible effect upon the *Edinburgh* results. A slightly stronger entry of twenty-four was received for this event, still confined only to motor-cycles and the second in the series. These included George Brough (Brough), W. W. Douglas (Douglas), D. S. Baddeley (Baddeley) – and Dr Moss-Blundell and H. Karslake on machines listed intriguingly as 'Own Make'; F. A. Hardy rode a $3^1/_2$hp Norton, 1909 being the first year in which a machine of this make had featured in an MCC Trial.

It appears that strip-map route-cards were issued for this event, and possibly earlier events, for on one section the mileage and time-allowance failed to tally, with disastrous effects upon the results. After much midnight oil-burning, F. G. Smith ($3^1/_2$hp Triumph) was sorted out as the winner of the Jarrott Cup, and 11'Golds', 3 'Silvers' and a single 'Bronze' were awarded. Douglas didn't do the Club's name much good, being reported as having behaved 'in a very noisy and disorderly manner' in the hotel used as the Penzance rest-halt; he was threatened – in writing – with exclusion from future events if he didn't conduct himself in a 'gentlemanly manner' in the years ahead. Douglas had had plenty of time in which to misbehave himself for, instead of the meagre six hours' rest allowed at Penzance during the first-ever *Land's End*, this rest period had been increased to a day and two nights for 1909. Of the 24 starters, 16 finished; the same route was used as for the 1908 event, via Salisbury, Exeter, Launceston, Bodmin, Truro and Penzance.

On New Year's Eve 1909, the sporting programme was drawn up for 1910, ambitious as ever. To this were added a host of social runs and gatherings of all sorts, from a smoking concert to the annual dinner.

March 12	Opening Run	June 4	Brooklands Race Meeting
March 25–28	Easter Run	June 18	Inter-Team Trial
March 25–28	London-Land's End-London	June 23	12-Hour Trial (motor-cycles)
April 30	Members' Hill-Climb	June 25	Fuel-Consumption Trial
May 13–16	London-Edinburgh-London	Sept 10	Members' Hill Climb
May 28	Albert Brown Trophy Trial		

The manner in which the London-Exeter-London came about – the third of the three MCC classic trials – indicates either how easy it was to set-up a long distance event in those days, or the remarkable organising powers of the club officials. At the committee meeting on 26 September 1910 someone asked : 'Mr Chairman, why don't we run a long-distance winter event?' – to which the almost unanimous reply was: 'Why not?' A post-card was sent to all members, letting them know of the proposal, to which a substantial number replied, expressing full approval. Initially it was proposed to run a winter-time *Edinburgh* but the Westcountry was eventually chosen in view of the milder winters; and the date was announced for 26 and 27 December 1910 – the very same year!

Unlike the *Edinburgh* and *Land's End*, the *Exeter* was a free-for-all from the start, admitting motor-cycles, cyclecars, and cars of any price or size. Entries consisted of 75 motor-cycles, 1 cyclecar (H. F. S. Morgan's Morgan three-wheeler) and 2 cars (V. H. Birch-Reynoldson's 10hp single-cylinder Cadillac, and C. M. Smith's 15.9hp 4-cylinder Thames). Starting from the Bell Hotel at Hounslow, the route ran down the old A30 through Salisbury, Yeovil and Honiton to Exeter – and back along the same route, a total distance of 322 miles to be completed to schedule throughout, and in twenty-four hours to qualify for a 'Gold'. In effect, it was identical to the first half of the early Land's End trials, and included no particularly troublesome hills; but predictably bad weather, the organisers reckoned, and the possible excitement of ice and snow, would provide hazards enough.

It must have been of enormous satisfaction to H. F. S. Morgan that his three-wheeler should have won a 'Gold' on this, its competition debut. It was only in 1910 that he had started marketing the production version of his Morgan Runabout, produced in association with W. Stephenson-Peach, engineering master at Malvern College, and with backing from Richard Burbridge, managing director of Harrods of Knightsbridge, who undertook to help sell the vehicle. Little did H. F. S. know that his tricycle brainchild was quickly to become an integral part of all MCC trials – later in four-wheeled form – and to develop into the world's most popular three-wheeler, taking part in an almost incredible number and variety of sporting events and providing a logical stepping-stone in the progress from solo motor-cycle to family car, right through until World War II and on until 1952.

By now, there were no fewer than 86,414 motor-cycles registered on the roads of Britain, and presumably contributing to the ever-growing Road Fund. Further contributing to the country's funds, Britain's motor-cycle industry was to export 3,418 machines during the year. So much for the 'Cinderella of our wheel trade' as the *Daily Mail* had described the motor-cycle in 1905.

In drawing up the regulations for the 1910 Inter-Team competition, the Committee agreed that no pedalling should be allowed in this event for 1910 – which must have meant that several competitors whose machines still depended upon 'L.P.A.' would have had to give up the event. Propriety was still splendidly high in the Club's list of attributes. In this event, the MCC finished second to the Sutton Coldfield AC, and information was received that *The Motor Cycle* magazine was proposing to award Silver Medals to the second-placed team, in addition to their principal award for the winner. It was agreed by the main Committee (who now met fortnightly, so busy was their schedule) that the MCC, as organisers of the event, should be the arbiters of what lesser prizes should be available, and to whom they should be awarded. *The Motor Cycle's* offer was politely declined.

For the Brooklands meeting, it was decided that only non-members of the Club should be required to pay entry fees (set at one shilling, or 5p) – which, despite the paltry sum, raised £26 12s 6d, suggesting an entry of well over 500, in addition to members. It was not until well into the thirties that figures approaching this became normal for the MCC trials. Together with admission charges, this brought the total takings for the meeting to £39 4s 10d. After payment of Mappin and Webb's bill (£20-odd) for trophies, hire of the track (£25), printing (£9-odd) and an expense account of £3 4s 6d submitted by Bidlake on behalf of the organising committee, this left a deficit of 'not much more than £23'.

Women were not yet regarded as equals. The application for membership from a Miss Behrend was 'deferred for the present', the decision being taken that '. . .the lady be written to and told that the Committee were reluctant to elect lady members'. This seems an odd decision in view of the successes already achieved by women drivers in MCC trials, notably Miss Muriel Hind (now Mrs Lord) who, along with others, must have been admitted on condition that they were driving (or riding) vehicles entered by members.

The demand for compliance with the law – then, as now – was strong. Rex Mundy's entry for the 1910 *Edinburgh* was firmly turned down on several grounds; that his entry had appeared in the Press before being accepted by the Club – which it would not have been anyway, because his licence had been suspended by Chester-le-Street magistrates for excessive speed in the 1908 *Edinburgh*, in addition to 'the large number of convictions against him for excessive speed'. How long, one wonders, did he have to wait before being able to expunge his misdeed in the 1908 *Edinburgh*?

Chapter 1 mentions the extraordinary 'brand loyalty' that has existed among

1913: With only external-contracting band-brakes and negligible stopping power when wet, the descents – such as this, on Trow Hill during a Jarrott Cup (*Land's End*) – were almost more intimidating than the observed climbs.

members through many, many years for the MCC events. In later chapters we shall see the same names recurring, year after year, through the thirties and into the sixties – and even much later – sometimes the same person, sometimes passing on from father to son, and even daughter. Already, by World War I when the Club was only thirteen years old, this trend was strong, with a few of the same names featuring in every event, right back to the beginning, many of them occurring with great regularity in the lists of award-winners.

The development of the *Land's End* up to the onset of WWI – and afterwards – is so typical of the thinking behind the three MCC 'classics' that it is worth going into in some detail since it was to become, for fairly obvious reasons, probably the best-known and most popular long-distance trial in motor-sporting history. It ran – and still runs – not only through the most densely-populated southern areas of England, but on into the far Westcountry where motor-cycles and cars – let alone large assemblies of them – were much less familiar; and there were still high glamour and romance in long-distance road travel, a fascination that was to continue for many years. As a result, thousands of spectators – arriving, even, in organised charabanc loads – gathered (and still gather) on the 'observed sections'.

The date set for the 1910 event, third in the series, was brought forward from August Bank Holiday to the Easter Weekend, starting a tradition that was to last until the present day, with the *Exeter* on Boxing Day (to be changed to early January in later years), the *Land's End* at Easter, and the *Edinburgh* at Whitsun. The route for the 1910 event was the same as for the previous two years, through Salisbury, Exeter, Launceston, Bodmin and Penzance – along the old A30, in fact, and back to London by the same route. Down through the Westcountry, though, the A30 was very different from today's wide and fairly straight main road, with its stretches of dual-carriageway. It was twisting, poorly-surfaced and very narrow. Cars and motor-cycles were scarce indeed – scarcer by far than horse-drawn carts with their ever-present plague of horse-shoe nails, shed on the roads to puncture the narrow, skinny 'pneumatic tyres' of man's latest inventions. Some idea of the road conditions that existed – even in the thirties – can be obtained from the few winding, narrow loops of the old road that still remain, where they have been 'straight-lined' and left as decaying reminders of long ago.

The 1910 event was still confined to motor-cycles, and was won by that sporting sailor Sir R. K. Arbuthnot, (see Appendix 3) – now Rear-Admiral – who was awarded the Jarrott Cup for his there-and-back performance on a $3^1/_2$hp Triumph. Again, though, the entry was nothing like that of the *Edinburgh* which was regularly attracting world-record entries for any motor-sporting event. In later years, the *Land's End* was to overtake even the

A *Land's End* competitor pauses for breath at Stoney Cross.

Edinburgh, with entries exceeding 500 for three successive years, the mixed column of cars and motor-cycles taking betwen nine and ten hours to pass through each of many 'observed sections' – a free-of-charge bonanza for the spectators.

Until – and including – the 1910 event, awards were allocated on the basis of time errors – early or late – at controls and secret checks spaced out along the route. For 1911 a more difficult route was chosen over Dartmoor through Moretonhampstead and Two Bridges, introducing the first 'observed sections' – mere hummocks by today's standards, but rough and stony then, thick with dust in dry weather and deep mud in the wet, providing very little grip for the narrow-section, high-pressure tyres. The new route decimated the field, fewer than half the 73 starters reaching Land's End on the outward journey.

Tough though it was, the special appeal for the *Land's End* among competitors was to increase. There was the onset of Spring in the Westcountry, with the woods in the Devon valleys a hazy, green mist of buds, and echoing to the 'tuff-tuff' of hard-worked engines; and there were the primroses lining the banks. There was, too, the exciting feeling of achievement for those who made it 'clean' to the end of an observed section, with the smell of Devon's red mud baking on hot exhaust pipes as riders rested after their exertions and allowed the machinery to cool down.

The route for the 1912 event was further stiffened, taking in the Ashburton, Holne Chase, Dartmeet and Two Bridges sections over Dartmoor. Though only 44 qualified for awards, out of 86 starters, Harold Karslake's achievement on a $3^1/_2$hp Rover in recording a total error of only fifty-two seconds for the entire double journey to win the Jarrott Cup indicates that the event's demands were far from insuperable. P. W. Moffatt, on a $2^3/_4$hp Douglas, won the special prize for lightweight machines, with an error of 1min 2sec, and Frank Smith the sidecar award on a 5-6hp Clyno; 26 'Golds' were awarded, and 15 'Silvers'.

It is interesting to note that it was in 1912 that the infamous Beggars' Roost, in North Devon, was first used as a trials hill – by the ACU in their Six Days' Trial. It was not until 1922 that it was first included in the route for the Land's End Trial, to be used annually ever since. 'Doctored' or not by the locals, it has become one of the MCC 's most formidable 'stoppers', especially in wet weather, and a name that will for ever be associated with the Club. The price for a gallon of petrol in those happy days was 1s $2^1/_2$d (roughly 6p today), recently increased from 9d; £1-odd would buy enough petrol for the entire trial!

The *Daily Express* offered a special cup in 1913 for the best performance using benzole fuel – a forlorn hope, since such petrol as was available along the route was stored in two-gallon cans at very infrequent filling-stations. In fact, even by 1923, when the first Le Mans 24-hours was held, competitors were required to complete 20×10.72-mile laps between refuelling-stops – a distance considered comparable to that between main-road filling-stations at the time. The *Daily Express* offer had to be declined; the task of distributing benzole was considered impossible.

It was inevitable, sooner or later, that cars would be admitted to the *Land's End*, though history does not record why this decision was not taken until 1914 – especially since they had been competing in the *Edinburgh* since 1906, eight years previously, and the first-ever *Exeter* in 1910. It may, perhaps, give an indication of road conditions in the far West, with the organisers regarding them as unsuitable for anything bulkier than a motor-cycle. The 1914 event was opened to light cars and cyclecars not exceeding 1,500cc, 36 cars taking part in a total entry of 174. Apart from many makes long-since forgotten, these included four 8hp Humberettes, three 10hp Morris Oxfords, three 8hp Morgan three-wheelers (previously admitted to the passenger-carrying motor-cycle classes), two 10hp ACs, an 11hp Lagonda and a 10hp Singer. The Lagonda was driven by W. H. Oates, later Major Oates who drove Lagondas at Brooklands in the twenties, and not to be confused with Dick Oats, who drove mainly OMs. Rex Mundy drove one of the ACs; R. F. Messervy, later of Rolls-Royce fame, a 10hp de P. Duo; and Lionel Martin, co-founder of Aston Martin, the popular little Singer, regarded by many as the prototype of subsequent light cars.

Thus, the pattern was set, with the three MCC classic events firmly established: the London-Edinburgh-London at Whitsun, first held in 1904, and opened to cars in 1906; the London-Land's End-London at Easter, first held in 1908 and opened to cars in 1914; and the London-Exeter-London on Boxing Day, first held in 1910 and admitting cars right from the start – plus, of course, the Brooklands Meeting in the summer, the Inter-Team Trial shortly after Brooklands, and many lesser competitive event, club runs and social gatherings. Entries for all three trials steadily increased; and, as cars became more dependable, official cars preceded competitors along the routes, their occupants – along with the 'travelling marshals' who mixed-it with competitors throughout the route – wearing 'bunches of green ribbons' to identify them. Prior to that, officials had travelled by rail to man the various controls and checks. Motor-cycle competitors wore numbered armbands on both arms – and all were advised, in the regulations, that 'It is a matter of courtesy not to annoy residents along the route'.

The first major change in the itinerary for the *Edinburgh* came in 1913, when the Scotch Corner, Penrith, Carlisle, Moffatt route replaced the original route to the east with its checks at Grantham, Wetherby, Durham, Berwick and Levenhall. In those days, the Penrith-Carlisle stretch was probably the fastest eighteen miles in the country, providing the officials with splendid opportunities for penalising competitors for speeding. The double-journey format was continued for the 1914 event.

The *Exeter*, too, was being progressively stiffened-up, as vehicle performance and reliability improved, and long distances alone became less of a problem. In 1912, the return journey was re-routed through Lyme Regis, Dorchester, and Blandford – 'A very severe route', as one motoring journal described it. It became even more difficult in 1913, when Chard and Trow hills had to be climbed non-stop. By now, the event had become firmly established with 231 entries, 65 of which were cars. There was no *Exeter* in 1914, though the *Land's End* and *Edinburgh*, together with the Brooklands meeting and other established annual events, continued until the onset of World War I.

All three trials – especially the *Exeter*, coming so soon after the Motor Show – gave manufacturers the opportunity of showing-off their new models, and more and more 'names' appeared in the entry lists. Not only were there the hardened campaigners Victor Riley, with his 12hp Rileys, George Brough who won the *Motor Cycle* Challenge Cup with his Brough in 1910, and H. F. S. Morgan with his Morgan Runabouts, but in 1912 W. E. Rootes (later Sir William) rode Singer motor-cycle No. 48 in the *Edinburgh*; and in 1913 William Morris (later Lord Nuffield) drove a 10hp Morris Oxford, winning a 'Gold' for the double run, along with W. E. Rootes (and, incidentally, appearing in the programme as 'W. R. Norris', driving a 'Norris-Oxford', which can't have pleased him much). In a Press interview, following his success, Rootes said: 'Participation in motoring sport is grand training for anyone who wants to become an expert driver. One never loses the feeling of confidence and road sense it engenders.'

Not only did the events provide manufacturers with 'exposure' for their products, but there was the successful advertising too, the extent of which indicates the status achieved by these events. In the 10 June 1914 issue of *The Light Car* (which cost one penny) the AC company bought the front cover, advertising that in the *Edinburgh* three ACs had started, and three finished the double journey –'Price £175, fully equipped'. Morgan Adler (nothing to do with 'H. F. S.'), Marshall Arter and Morris-Oxford bought whole pages inside the journal, to advertise that they had won 'Golds'; and Arden, La Ponette and Sirron half-pages or less. The six-car Morris-Oxford team, entered by Stewart and Arden, in completing the double journey intact, won the Silver Cup for Best Performance along with six Gold Medals. A seventh Morris-Oxford, too, won a 'Gold', equalling the performance by seven Humbers, though these were evidently not entered as a team.

CHAPTER 3

First Re-start

By the time of the Armistice on 11 November 1918, the development of cars and motor-cycles had advanced so quickly in the forcing-ground of war that reliability had become almost a *fait accompli* under normal road conditions. There was no further purpose, therefore, in putting it to the test by means of the 'there-and-back', main-road long distances of pre-war days. There arose the need to test the 'capability' – not only of the vehicles themselves, but of their riders/drivers too – under less normal, or even abnormal conditions. The 'and-back' element was soon dropped from all three events, with the single, outward routes taking to minor roads, and making occasional sorties into the testing conditions of off-road farm tracks, bridle paths, pack-horse lanes and suchlike. Many of these were to become firmly established through the years in the long list of famous trials hills that are now an inseparable part of the Exeter, Land's End and Edinburgh trials (See Appendix 6). In short, the term 'reliability trial' became redundant – or at least part-redundant – the whole character of the events becoming more 'sporting'. There was still, however, no element of speed in these events, the old system of time controls and secret checks along the route being maintained, to ensure that competitors kept to the very leisurely schedule. In fact, there appeared on the programme for the first post-war *Edinburgh* that famous MCC announcement 'This event is not a race' – to be retained on all three programmes for many years afterwards.

The early introduction of such frightening ascents as Porlock and Lynton hills in the Westcountry, under the heading 'Observed Sections' started this

A PASSENGER'S DREAM:

THE NIGHT BEFORE THE "LAND'S END."

1927: It was the dream of most boys to compete in the MCC trials – a dream that was encouraged by this awe-inspiring 'artist's impression' of the Land's End Trial (by F. Gordon Crosby, of course) in *The Boys' Book of Motor-cycling*.

BLUEHILLS MINE IN THE LONDON—LAND'S END TRIAL.

(Top, Left) D. F. Still (A.B.C.) stopped on the hairpin and slipped back before proceeding. (Right) Another unlucky competitor was B. W. Harcourt, whose Austin charged the bank as a result of taking the corner too fast. (Bottom) An outstanding performance was made by V. G. Wallsgrove (Riley).

1924: Unfettered by considerations of dead-accuracy, Gordon Crosby was able to portray far more in these 'impressions' of incidents during the Land's End Trial than the camera ever could! And how much more exciting he made *The Autocar*'s reports for their readers.

trend – their surfaces being as much of a problem as their gradients, many of them being similar, then, to today's Litton Slack, Beggars' Roost and others. And 'Non-stop' didn't simply mean climbing the hill without stopping – but doing so from a standing-start at the beginning of the gradient, with no chance of building-up engine revs and speed to rush the hill.

It is not easy today to appreciate how difficult such a test could be for some of the low-powered vehicles of the day. To the accompaniment of clouds of smoke and acrid smells from overheated clutch linings, they would start to move forward – only to falter to a halt as the clutch became fully engaged and engine speed fell to a tick-over. In the wet, when the surfaces were appallingly muddy, it might be possible to induce wheelspin, and maintain engine speed in the range where at least a little torque was being developed; but it required great skill to balance wheelspin against forward movement until road speed – and consequently engine torque – made the ascent possible. In the dry it might be necessary to slip the clutch for a considerable distance, until road speed built up to match the range of reasonable engine torque but, as often as not, the clutch lining had burned out by then. Even in far less demanding conditions, where there was ample room to 'rush' it, I can remember drivers depositing their passengers at the foot of our local, 1 in 6 half-mile hill in Cornwall, while they coaxed their unburdened cars to the summit, picking up the passengers when they arrived.

Getting moving quickly after the Armistice, the committee (still with Charles Jarrott as president, until 1922) met on 11 December 1918 to draw up a tentative programme for 1919. There was no time to set up the Land's End Trial for Easter, but the evening of 6 June 1919 saw the familiar (though small) gathering at Ye Olde Gatehouse, Highgate Hill, north London, with the *Edinburgh* ahead of them. Not only had the route been stiffened, and the return journey dropped, but women drivers and riders had been banned from the event, a curious decision in view of the part women had played as despatch-riders and ambulance-drivers during the war.

Competitors were sent off at half-mile intervals, starting at 9pm, the organisers claiming as a bonus point that, in view of the Daylight Saving Act, they would start in broad daylight and enjoy at least one hour's run before it was completely dark, taking them to Hatfield. They also stated that Mr H. J. C. Spring, proprietor at Ye Olde Gatehouse, had undertaken to provide supper for competitors from 6.30 to 8.45pm, and that he was prepared to fill vacuum flasks with hot coffee and to provide sandwiches. The same facilities were available at the first stop, at The Swan Hotel, Biggleswade and at the garage in Grantham. In such places as York (2nd breakfast stop) and Carlisle (lunch) it would, they said, be a case of first come, first served. 'This will help

THE PORLOCK ASCENT.

1922: *The Autocar's* famous artist Freddy Gordon Crosby records an exciting moment on Porlock during the Land's End Trial, when G. W. Lucas in a Riley had to do some quick thinking to avoid J. R. Oliver's Alvis which had stalled, run backwards, and blocked the road.

the solo riders (as it's right that it should) since they have no accommodation for luncheon baskets. All alcohol should be eschewed during the event', they advised, 'though perhaps a little light wine at dinner before the start would do no harm.' A whole paragraph was given over to reminding competitors not to forget to wind up and set their watches before the start. Such old-world solicitude is no longer included in the regulations. Seventy-five per cent of the entry won Gold Medals.

The *Exeter*, too, was held in 1919, again on 26 and 27 December, retaining the 'and back' element. Of the 148 entries (many of them presumably dating from pre-war), 126 set off from the Bridge Hotel, Staines, in a blinding rain-storm that continued all night. Most of the entries were still running to schedule at the first time check, the White Hart Hotel, Salisbury.

Road conditions between Wilton and Yeovil were described by R. Crick-Davis (Chater-Lea and sidecar) in *The Motor Cycle*: 'Conditions were atrocious. I gave up trying to steer clear of the pot-holes in the hope that this way I might miss more than I would by deliberate steering; and, as nothing worked loose or broke, perhaps I was justified in that hope . . .I never had a sidecar skid about so much in all my long experience.'

Trojans have always been popular, and successful, in MCC trials. This one is making its stately and sure-footed way to Land's End, almost obscured by the enormous crowd of warmly-clad spectators – and the ubiquitous AA Scout.

1925: The MCC's Inter-Club Team Trial always drew good entries and provided keen competition. Here Freddy Jones, of the Sheffield and Hallamshire club's team, urges his Morgan forward while his passenger greets an old acquaintance.

The first observed, non-stop section was Chard Hill, generally managed easily; and, still ascending through Yarcombe, the route led through Honiton to the Bude Hotel at Exeter, whence the return journey went via Sidford to the second non-stop section at Trow Hill – which was attempted on the run. In consequence, there were sometimes three or four competitors struggling on the hill at the same time, producing – inevitably – a degree of chaos. With no further observed sections, the route ran along the south coast through Dorchester, though a secret check three miles before Blandford cost quite a few their Gold Medals, and through Salisbury to the finish. So uneventful and monotonous was this final part of the journey that Jackie Masters – among many others – dawdled away the time to arrive just 120 seconds early. He hadn't the patience he said '. . .to swank in, dead on time'.

Of the 31 solo motor-cycles to start the event, 26 finished; 45 of the 62 sidecar outfits, and 24 of the 33 cars also completed the trial. In their reports, *The Autocar* referred to the latter as Light Cars, *The Light Car* as Cyclecars; and *The Motor Cycle* as Runabouts! Among the finishers were J. A. Masters, Rex Mundy, 'Sammy' Davis, D. W. Hawkes and Kaye Don.

It was in 1920 that the club returned fully to normal, with a programme of sporting and social events. The *Land's End* was held at Easter with tightened-up regulations and including non-stop climbs of the previously mentioned Porlock and Lynton hills. The total distance was 314 miles, starting from the White Hart Hotel at Cranford Bridge, Hounslow, and finishing at the Land's End Hotel. Though Porlock is much longer than Lynton, its average gradient is 1 in 6, compared with Lynton's 1 in 5, with a steepest stretch of 1 in 4 and, for this event, a muddy, stony surface throughout, whereas Porlock had wintered well. As each competitor passed the summit of Porlock there were anxious glances at route cards as the ensuing thirteen miles to Lynton had to be covered precisely at a regular average speed of 15mph – a stretch which included winding lanes across Exmoor and the long, steep descent of Countisbury Hill. The north Devon roads were appalling; in describing them, one report says: 'The war-battered roads of France, or even those of Belgium, and particularly the one from Poperinghe to Ypres, can be equalled, it seems, in England as considerable stretches of the road from Lynton Hill to Barnstaple, and thence to Holsworthy, were in an awful condition.'

1927: Major Reggie Marians, long-serving and popular MCC official, at Brighton making one of his rare appearances as a competitor, rather than an official, in a Club event.

There were 161 starters, of which 70 were solo motor-cycles, 65 sidecars and three-wheelers, and 26 'small cars' – not one of which was a saloon. Of these, 58 solos completed the route (80 per cent of the solo starters), 43 sidecars and three-wheelers (65 per cent), and 18 small cars (69 per cent); a total of 117 finished (72 per cent). Among the 14 car drivers to qualify for Gold Medals were Lionel Martin (Aston Martin), Major W. H. Oates (Lagonda), S. C. H. ('Sammy') Davis (driving an air-cooled ABC), C. M. Harvey (Eric Campbell), C. Finch (GN), Kaye Don and Victor Bruce (ACs), C. T. Newsome (air-cooled Rover), and A. Frazer Nash (GN). To those who followed motor sport in subsequent years, these names were to become very familiar indeed.

'Sammy' Davis wrote of the event in a contemporary issue of *The Autocar*: 'Even the start at Cranford Bridge was different, for, beside the usual scene of flaring lamps, the reek of carbide from the motor-cycles, and exhaust smoke, and the crowd of weirdly apparelled men, almost every car carried Parsons chains as a tribute to the formidable powers of Porlock and Lynton; and round these chains centred much argument.

'Oates and Lionel Martin already had theirs on spare wheels ready to fit, but on the ABC we carried a bag of chains and rehearsed so vigorously that barely four minutes sufficed to stop, fit chains, and restart.' He goes on to say that, later in the trial '. . .the crew of the ABC were greatly uplifted by receiving hot-cross-buns, hurled into the car as it passed through Glastonbury by a representative of the Tor Cycle and Motor Company – a very kindly act'.

Also quoting 'Sammy' Davis, this time from his book *Motor Racing* where he is discussing the MCC's long-distance trials: 'As an outlet for one's energies, either before or in conjunction with motor racing, I have always found the more exciting of the road trials . . .extremely satisfactory. And they bear on the question of racing more, perhaps, in my case than any other, simply because they give one a good, sound training, both in the preparation of the car and in driving before a crowd of spectators among a crowd of other cars.' Perhaps this explains why, in the twenties and thirties, so many famous British racing drivers used regularly to take part in the MCC trials, especially the *Exeter* and *Land's End*, during the close season of racing. Sadly, this is no longer the case, with professional racing drivers competing in events only upon payment of very considerable sums of money, and the sport – if it is still a sport – is greatly the poorer for it.

'Sammy' goes on to say: 'That excellent body, The Motor Cycling Club, has provided the enthusiast with more fun for less money than any other club, I think, in the world. In the old days, the London-Edinburgh really was a trial . . .It was at its best on a motor-cycle . . .as, for example, when I pedalled practically all the way from Highgate to York, in which town collapse from

1927: L. W. G. Skinner takes a wide line around the old Bluehills Mine hairpin on his EW Douglas in the *Land's End*. This part of the hill is now metalled and in use daily.

fatigue was inevitable. The engine, it is true, ran the whole way; but, as it hadn't enough power to pull the skin off a rice pudding, that merely made things worse.'

Spare a moment to pity the poor historian. . . . In his excellent 'History' articles in the MCC's magazine *Triple*, that great authority H. W. Tucker-Peake writes: 'The statement "The Exeter Trial, first run in 1910. . ." is often used and is quite incorrect. The title "Exeter Trial" was not used until 1930. From the start in 1910 it was known as the "Winter Club Run", with the sub-heading "London to Exeter and back for Motor Cycles, Sidecar Machines, Cycle Cars and Cars". . .'

However, in their report of the 1920 event, *The Light Car and Cyclecar* (1 January 1921) opens with the words: 'The London-Exeter Trial this year has demonstrated . . .' Yer pays yer money. . .but to most of us it will always be simply the *Exeter* – from 1910 until the present day.

The 1920 event, starting at Staines and still retaining the return run, was generally agreed to have been too easy – in the light of the improved reliability and efficiency of what were by then almost entirely post-war vehicles. *The Light*

1927: F. W. A. Cooper, taking part in the Land's End Trial on his Zenith (remember the gate on their back mudguard, indicating they were barred from racing?). Allegedly only fourteen years old at the time, Cooper was certainly the youngest entry.

1927: As well as bad weather, in the London-Exeter's luck-of-the-draw, there is always the possibility of rain-swollen watersplashes – such as this one, in the wilds of Dorset, with L. Bates trying not to douse his Ariel's ignition.

Car's report states: 'Curious to relate, we did not come across any competitors stopped at the roadside until we reached Hartford Bridge Flats. This surprised us considerably. . .'. Only one car failed on Trow Hill, whereas in 1919 the failures had been heavy. The terrors of Chard Hill were overshadowed by intimidating reports of a newcomer, Peak Hill, though they seem to have been unfounded. 'Particularly fast ascents', *The Light Car* records, 'were made by Capt Frazer Nash's G. N., and the whole fleet of Morgans which came up like streaks of lightning' (3-wheelers, of course). Again, the entry included names that were to become household words in the sport: the Hon Victor Bruce (10hp AC), S. C. H. Davis (12hp ABC), W. H. Oates (11hp Lagonda), R. G. Jackson (10hp GWK), C. M. Harvey (10hp Eric Campbell), R. G. Mundy (7hp De Marcay), and many others, cutting their teeth on MCC events.

At that time, and right through until World War II, the weekly journals *The Motor Cycle, Motor Cycling, The Autocar, The Motor* and *The Light Car* published extensive guides to the three classic trials, including entry lists and maps showing locations of the observed sections and the time of arrival at each of them by the first (motor-cycle) competitor – a service much appreciated (and one that still would be) by the thousands of spectators that turned out to watch. For the 1921 *Land's End* there were 216 entries, including 69 light cars and cycle-cars, the remaining 147 being made up of solo motor-cycles and sidecar outfits, and only three large cars (two Morris Oxfords and a Westwood), indicating a very active motor-cycle and small car interest. Principal tests were the ascent of Porlock at a stipulated average of not less than 18mph, and the twelve miles from the foot of Porlock to the top of Lynton Hill that had to be completed at 20mph; a late limit of five minutes was set.

The car entry included seven Rovers, six Morgans, six GNs, four GWKs, four ABCs, four ACs, three Lagondas, and three Cardens. Other makes represented were: TB Tricar, Coventry Premier, Castle Three, AV, Tamplin, Silver Hawk, Unit No. 1, Victor, Aston Martin, Riley, Orpington, Secqueville-Hoyau, Baughan, Calthorpe, Swift, McKenzie, Douglas, Charron-Laycock, De Marcay, Warren-Lambert, Hillman, Surrey, Singer, Hotchkiss, Kings-

1927: A. Shaw's New Hudson takes a tight line on the hairpin of the old Bluehills – with an impressive backdrop showing the old mine workings from which this famous MCC 'stopper' takes its name. The hill is now leased by the Club.

In laying-on their Winter Trial – the London-Exeter – the Club invited bad weather, and frequently got it. Here are two competitors, led by W. Gray on his Dunelt Monarch, picking their muddy way through a corner on Little Minterne.

bury, Morris Oxford and Westwood. Of these, only Rover, Morgan and Aston Martin survive.

'A London-Edinburgh Without Parallel!' headed one of the journals' accounts of the 1921 event, held as usual at Whitsun; and the writer went on to wonder '. . .if ever before have so many people congregated at one time in the vicinity of Ye Olde Gate House, at Highgate . . .'to see off the 400-odd starters, 268 of which were solos and sidecar outfits, and 132 cars. 'A novel type of windscreen clearer adorned Mr S. H. Roe's early model AC,' the writer said. 'It is an electrical contrivance and is, we understand, particularly efficacious.' What is more, about half the motor-cycle entry had electric lighting – and two cars (all of which, it seems, were open) were fitted with sidescreens. Buttertubs Pass, with a surface not unlike many of today's trial hills, was included in the route.

The *Light Car* headed its preview of the 1922 *Land's End* 'The Most Strenuous English 24-Hour Trial Ever Organised', and sub-titled its report 'One of the most instructive 24-hour events ever held'. Heavy rain, sleet, gale-force headwinds and flying twigs contributed to the hazards on the 400-mile route – and Beggars' Roost appeared for the first time on the route cards. The stipulated average up Porlock was reduced from 18 to 15mph for cars over 1,100cc, and 12mph for the motor-cycles and small cars. The Westcountry hills had been deep in snow a week before the event. 'Should these conditions prevail on Saturday', one of the journals wrote, 'it is more than likely that some exceedingly spectacular work will be seen!'.

By now the various reports were crediting the *Edinburgh* with being the most popular of the three trials, being held in predictably fair weather at Whitsun, and including none of the 'freak' hills that made the *Land's End* the toughest. No fewer than twenty three-wheelers took part in the 1922 event, eleven of them Morgans, and one a Scott Sociable, that curious 'land-crab' produced by the Scott company at Shipley. A couple of years later, one of these ran in the *Edinburgh* 'four-up', the little 600cc, water-cooled, twin-cyclinder two-stroke finishing successfully, though it boiled on Kirkstone.

It was still the London-Exeter-London in 1922, eighth of the series and starting on Boxing Night from the Bridge House Hotel at Staines – described with remarkable foresight by a contemporary reporter as '. . .one of the greatest pastimes in which interest will never flag'. The asides by some of the journalists make charming reading. . . .Two new hills were included: Salcombe (just outside Sidmouth), and the long, chalky White Sheet, near Beaminster. Of the former it is recorded, in describing the start: 'Some there were who knew Salcombe, and who sagely nodded their heads, breathing in sepulchral voices "Chains!". Others, ignorant of the locality, shrugged their

1925: The value of the long-distance MCC events to manufacturers in publicising their products is all too clear in this group of motor-cyclists at the start of the London-Edinburgh – the limelight being hogged by George Brough in this case!

shoulders and declared they would be governed in their actions by the conditions prevailing when the battlefield was reached'. Small wonder the reports ran to five or six pages.

First mention of Simms as a trial hill occurs in the *Light Car* of 16 February 1923, in their account of a hill-climb organised by that journal in which only nine of the thirty-seven competitors climbed the hill. The name 'Sibbs Hill' has sometimes been used in the distant past for this steep lane leading up to the edge of Dartmoor – explained in the *Light Car*'s report by the fact that the man who had discovered and christened it the previous autumn had been suffering from a severe head-cold! It was not until eleven years later that the hill was to appear (as Simms) in an *Exeter*, when it was described in a subsequent report as being 'almost unclimbable'.

As the 1920s progressed, entries in the *Exeter* and *Land's End* increased steadily, as did the publicity accorded to them – with the British motor-cycle and car makers taking advantage of this by entering works' teams. The *Exeter* especially provided an excellent shop window for people in far-flung places who had not been able to visit the car and motor-cycle shows in London. The start of the 1924 *Exeter* at Staines was actually broadcast. Of this technological breakthrough, one of the journals wrote: 'Suddenly, the familiar greeting "Hullo! Hullo! 2LO calling!" rising above the general babel in the street below focused 500 pairs of eyes on the balcony of Saltmarsh's Garage right opposite the starting point . . .many must have missed the four "loud-speakers" . . .owing to the dazzle, until the wireless voice spoke out. . . .We compliment the Westminster Radio Syndicate and Saltmarsh's Garage on an innovation which brought this year's start "bang up to date".' Many years after, in the late thirties, a BBC team consisting of Richard Dimbleby and Arthur Phillips set up shop on Beggars' Roost in the *Land's End*, describing the performances of the motor-cycles and cars.

For some odd reason the Society of Motor Manufacturers and Traders (SMM and T) placed a ban in 1926 on works' participation in these events, though the ACU did not apparently share their views so far as the motor-cycles were concerned. It was a year in which the entry for the *Exeter* was to reach a 425 record, 259 of which were motor-cycles and sidecar outfits. The start from close to Staines Bridge was moved for this event from the traditional Boxing

1926: Long time member of the Executive Committee and a Club Vice-President, Jack Davis – aged over eighty – is seen here taking part in his first-ever MCC event, the London-Edinburgh, on a 350cc Royal Enfield.

Night to 28 December – the motor-cycle entries attributing this to the fact that the car drivers required an extra couple of days to get over their Christmas excesses! The 336-mile route, still with the 'and back' element, included only four observed hills, all on the outward journey, compared with 13 in the 1989 event.

In reply to this *Exeter* record, the *Land's End* came up with no fewer than 530 entries for the 1926 event – 205 of them cars (including 20 three-wheelers) and 325 motor-cycles. The route included four observed hills – Porlock, Lynton, Beggars' Roost and Bluehills Mine. The *Edinburgh*, however, which reports had so recently claimed to be the most popular of the three, attracted only 87 cars for the 1926 event, of which 83 finished, 64 of them claiming First Class Awards. 'Is the *Edinburgh* getting too easy?' one of the journals asked. Subsequent experience has shown that the tougher the event, the greater the enjoyment for competitors – and that any suggestion of easing a section is invariably greeted by letters of protest.

Always a possible victim to the weather – though, incredibly, seldom proving to be so – the 1927 *Exeter* was well and truly snowed-off. Though there had been plenty of warnings, during the post-Christmas run-down to the start, that the event might have to be cancelled, it was not until the marshals set off on the Tuesday evening to man their controls and observed sections that they found the main road route from Staines completely blocked – with police warnings that Salisbury Plain was impassable. There was no time to inform competitors, who bravely turned up in force at the start, only to find the announcement, chalked on a blackboard, that the event was off. Somehow this 1927 non-event seems to sum up the spirit of adventure that exists in these long-distance, day-and-night events. As the evening passed, first the motor-cycles and then the cars continued hopefully to arrive, the motor-cyclists unsuccessfully trying to cope with the deeply-rutted snow, and mostly falling off. Under the floodlights they gathered, many of them prepared to have a go at an event of their own. Eventually, though, they agreed reluctantly to go home – but not before they had managed to find a band to play for them at the 'official' restaurant, where an impromptu dance was held. The costumes of the dancers, including the footwear of the motor-cycle contingent, on that bitter night can be imagined!

Reports of that year's *Land's End* indicate how development was progressing. Describing the event in general, a contemporary writer says: '. . .but a better surface and four-wheel brakes have now robbed it of its terrors, whilst four-wheel brakes have also made it possible to descend Countisbury Hill a good deal faster than of old.' A somewhat irresponsible attitude – and one that would not be countenanced today – crept into the writer's description of A. C. Maskell's ascent of Beggars' Roost in his Aero Morgan-JAP. 'He literally streaked up the hill,' the writer says; but during his meteoric ascent the steering column broke, whereupon the Morgan '. . .charged the bank, heeled over at an alarming angle and leapt across the road into the spectators . . .unfortunately a small boy was injured.' Undeterred by this disaster, the writer goes on to say: ' . . .Maskell told us that the speedometer was showing 42mph just before the accident – a really splendid performance!'

Contemporary accounts of these '. . .battles long ago' provide a remarkable social history of the times. At the start of the 1927 *Edinburgh*, one reporter states: 'Although the beret basque is now out of fashion, there was the usual assortment of strange headgear and quixotic attire. Several gramophones, carried in competing cars, made the evening hideous, blaring out various musical atrocities to the general disturbance of the nerves of many. . . .'

Askrigg was again the first observed section – known locally as Flow Edge – with a gulley on the steepest section, near the summit, dammed by locals to form a watersplash 6ft wide by 10in deep. Though the motor-cycles and sidecar outfits put up ' . . .many monotonous but excellent performances . . .', the car entry didn't fare so well because of a strong following wind which made the engines boil. The turnout of spectators at this and other observed sections prompted one writer to comment: 'It is clear that the MCC London-Edinburgh Run has not the same hold upon the public as the London-Land's End, or even the Exeter.'

The 1928 *Land's End* attracted the phenomenal entry of 553 – following 530 and 527 in 1926 and 1927. Roughly one-third of each of these were cars, the remainder being made up of solo motor-cycles, sidecar outfits, and three-wheelers. During the thirties, however, the balance swung strongly in the opposite direction, and in 1934, for example, there were 366 cars in the total entry of 465. This steady increase in car entries may well have been attributed to the fact that in 1925 the capacity limit for cars had been raised to 2,000cc (from 1,500cc), with a further increase to 3,000cc in 1927, and the present unlimited capacity, free-for-all in 1928. Jackie Masters, in his 'History of the Land's End' (*Autocar*, 7 September 1945) attributes this gradual admittance of the largest cars to the improvements in brakes and steering locks as well as general manoeuvrability. The use of snow-chains in this and other MCC events was banned in 1925.

CHAPTER 4

Enter Jackie Masters

It must have been in 1928 that I began to take a personal interest in the *Land's End* (the sixteenth in the series) when the old route left the A30 to run along Penzance promenade to Newlyn, up Paul (alias Chywoone) Hill very close to our home, and along ' . . .the final perfectly dreadful twelve miles to Land's End', as one report described it. With the family Chrysler parked as a grandstand among the hundreds of spectators, we children would sit eating hot-cross-buns and watching the weary, mud-encrusted procession climb 'our hill'. The entry that year was up to an impressive 553, including 260 solo motor-cycles, 37 Austin Sevens – and 23 Morgan three-wheelers, the lengthy procession of which fired my ambition one day to own one. This didn't come until 1935 (a 1925 Family two-seater) followed by a 1932 Super Sports (in 1937) and a 1936 Matchless-engined Super Sports in 1939 (now providing great pleasure for its owner in America) – with a first drive in the *Land's End* in 1939. These three Morgans cost respectively £1 10s, £37 and £62!

I remember, too, a man called D. M. Healey, driving a new Triumph Super Seven – already well known as a rally driver, and a local hero to us as he lived at Perranporth where he and his father ran a garage business. That year, for the first time, the route approached Bluehills Mine through Perranporth, the Healey family providing free cups of tea, coffee and light refreshments to competitors, a custom that continued for many years.

Among the memories of this and subsequent pre-World War II *Land's Ends* are the motoring journals' reports of the Easter Monday race-meetings

'Mr MCC'. Since its inception in 1901 there have been many great characters who have shaped the Club's history – but none who did more to maintain its efficiency and reputation than Jackie Masters – assisted always by his wife Bea.

at Brooklands, recording the fact that a few of the competing cars (notably H. J. Aldington's Frazer Nash, from memory) were still mud-stained and battle-scarred from the Land's End Trial, two days earlier. How better could the versatility of sporting cars be demonstrated?

The *Exeter* that year, thirteenth in the series and postponed until 13 January because of bad weather, was unaffected by the combination of 'unlucky 13s'; and the *Edinburgh* came of age with its twenty-first running – claimed by the Press to be 'The most interesting London-Edinburgh ever run so far'. By now, the illustrated accounts of these events show quite a few closed cars taking part – and the 1929 *Land's End* reports show pictures of the M-Type MG Midget making its trials debut with an Abingdon-sponsored team of four cars. Little, if anything, is made in the reports of the significance of this newcomer that was to continue in an unbroken line to the TF Midget of 1953, dominating the entry lists of so many events in the thirties. The little cars created a stir throughout the route; and when the four of them parked in line abreast at the Land's End Hotel, following the trial, the local interest was tremendous. By now, one assumes that the SMM and T had lifted their ban on factory participation in MCC trials.

Whatever may have been the views of the Press as to the nature of the *Exeter*, H. W. Tucker-Peake's claim that it did not become a 'trial' until the 1930 event (see previous chapter) is amply confirmed by *The Light Car*'s heading to their report: 'The "Exeter" as a Trial'. The sub-title goes on to say: 'Rain, Wind and New Hills Make MCC Classic Winter Run Justify Its New Title – "Trial".' Their report opens splendidly by quoting a remark by a female spectator at the Slough Trading Estate start – uttered whilst pointing at a Lea-Francis: 'My dear, how simply excruciatingly thrilling. I feel sure that lovely green Bugatti is going to win!'

Middledown (first used in 1920), Devenish Pit (new), Higher Rill (new), Harcombe, Meerhay (new), Batcombe (new) and Ibberton Church Hill (new) were the tough observed sections that justified the title of 'trial', and the return journey to London was abandoned. Thus, the *Exeter*, on its fifteenth running, fell into line with the *Land's End*; the *Edinburgh*, still something of a 'club run', was yet to be stiffened-up. This demanding route took a heavy toll of the 121 solo motor-cycles and sidecar outfits, especially the latter. The car entry reached 203, with 26 MG Midgets, 21 Frazer Nashes, 17 Austin Sevens, 11 Triumphs and 8 Ford V8s (all 30hp). And the entry list reads like a Who's Who of well-known drivers, with the Aldingtons (H. J. and D. A.), Tommy Wisdom, C. Penn-Hughes and the ever-smiling Neil Berry (racing driver and co-driver with 'H.J.' in so many big-time rallies) all driving Frazer Nashes. Added to these, were Hugh Hunter, Maurice Toulmin, C. F.

Dobson, Viscount Chetwynd, Sammy Davis, Jim Brymer (later to become a well known photographer of MCC events), Mike Couper, A. P. McGowan, K. J. Kehoe – and a host more. The following year, 1931, the *Exeter* entry list included Oliver Bertram in a 30/98 Vauxhall –along with a Talbot 90, Hillman Husky, Humber Snipe, $4^1/_2$-litre Invicta, $4^1/_2$-litre Bentley and several other big cars.

The *Edinburgh*'s turn for a face-lift came in 1931, the year that Jackie Masters (see Chapter 12) became trials organiser. Until well after World War II his familiar figure, clad in a checked tweed overcoat, and always accompanied by his wife Bea, was to be seen at most observed sections on every MCC trial, chatting with competitors and making sure all was well. To the existing list of hills – Fleet Moss, Askrigg, West Stonesdale and Tan Hill – he added

1939: Like dinosaurs, the Ford V8 specials appeared on the scene, multiplied, ruled the roost – and became extinct. Bertie Woodall looks apprehensive in his version, the front suspension of which seems to owe more to Morgan than Ford.

Middle Tongue (near Harrogate) and Park Rash (near Kettlewell). The latter was regarded as highly dangerous in Yorkshire, there were no incidents, but it stopped 76 entries. With this stiffening-up the *Edinburgh*, as the *Exeter* had done the year before, officially became a trial – however competitors and the Press may have regarded it during previous years! And, curiously, with this stiffening-up came a steady decline in the motor-cycle entries. Between the years 1931 and 1939, there was a total entry of 2,264 for this event – of which

1928: A very standard Riley saloon nears the summit of Porlock in the *Land's End*. Although nowadays a main road hill, even in recent years Porlock was regarded as an obstacle – and in the twenties it was still a real 'stopper'.

1935: International rally driver, Chief Constable of Northamptonshire, Captain of the BMC works rally team . . .John Gott (Singer Le Mans; at the Wrotham Park start of the *Land's End*) was typical of those who began successful careers by entering MCC events.

1,692 were cars and 572 were motor-cycles.

As a regular competitor himself from the MCC's early days, and for many years afterwards, Masters was vastly experienced and, under his guidance through the thirties and fifties, the MCC events reached what many people regard as their heyday. In 1931 he turned his attention to the *Land's End*, to which Grabhurst (near Dunster) and Ruses Mill (near Launceston) had been added the previous year. He introduced a limited speed test on Dunkery Beacon and Wells Head Hill – and the famous Hustyn, which produced 91 failures on its debut. He brought in Beggars' Roost in 1922 – still in use and probably the most famous of all the MCC hills – which stopped 88 competitors that year. To these he also added the top hairpin of Lynton in 1932, and Station Lane, extremely steep, but not too rough for those who took to the pavement. This practice was banned in 1933 – the year he introduced 'Gooseham' to his new-found list of stoppers. In fact, Gooseham was the name of the hill descended by competitors in order to reach the new observed section on the other side of the valley – which was to become another well-known

MCC hill through the years, under its correct name of Darracott.

Although the *Exeter* had already been upgraded in 1930, Masters turned his hand to this event, adding the popular and interesting Fingle Bridge in 1932, when the start was moved to Virginia Water and the finish to the Crown Hotel, Blandford. He added the infamous Simms in 1933, a year in which a record entry of 427 was received for the *Exeter*, 273 of them cars – of which 191 required the tractor's help to reach the summit of Simms. The year 1933 also marked one of Masters' most significant innovations – the introduction of team awards into the MCC trials. As Wilson McComb writes in his excellent article 'Trials and Tribulations' (*MG Enthusiast*, February/March 1985):

> Austin, Singer and MG were three prominent manufacturers who gave surreptitious backing to leading drivers, recognising that success in trials brought considerable publicity, and although this aroused much resentment among the private entrants, it became the done thing to run as a named team, each trio holding station and tackling the observed sections in number order, one after another. Austin had their 'Grasshoppers', Singer their impressively named 'Candidi Provocatores' and the cream-and-brown MGs of Toulmin, Macdermid and Bastock became the 'Cream Crackers' after the biscuits of that name.

There were also many, many private teams – the 'Jabberwock' Ford V8s and 'Nibelungs' Frazer Nashes among the many noteworthy names.

In the 1933 *Exeter*, Toulmin, Bastock and Taylor, driving MG J2 Midgets, won the team award – the only team to win three 'Golds' out of a total of only eighteen awarded among the 273 cars entered (eleven MGs, three Singers, two 30hp Ford V8s, a Frazer Nash and a Bugatti).

Whether or not the energetic and resourceful Jackie Masters was overdoing things in the Committee's opinion is not recorded, but at the 1933 AGM there was lengthy discussion about the rapidly increasing costs of running trials; and that on-going problem of whether women drivers should be permitted was again raised (and again shelved). And, once more, the advisability of a change in name was considered. 'Motorists don't like being members of a motor-cycling club!' was the cry – but 'A solid phalanx of Committee members, plus three sleepy ordinary members . . .' agreed to leave things as they were – which is as they still are today. For the first time, the possibility of banning competition tyres ('knobblies') was considered.

The ever tougher *Exeter* produced even more entries in 1934, with a new record of 296 cars out of a total of 364. Simms again played its part; 212 cars needed the tractor's help, and out of the record entry only 18 competitors qualified for Premier Awards. This time it was three 30hp Ford V8s that won the Team Award, driven by Viscount Chetwynd, G. M. Denton and J. B. Thompson – all three winning 'Golds'. The following year, 1935, there was a special award for climbing the dreaded Simms and, to the dismay of the Committee, 102 competitors claimed the award. This was owed, apparently, to the compassion of the contractors who yearly carried out surface repairs (at the Club's expense). A special Veteran Class was included in this event for those who had competed in the first *Exeter* 25 years before. George Brough, H. F. S. Morgan, L. A. Baddeley, B. Alan Hill, W. Cooper, Sam Wright, N. C. Dear, Rex Mundy and George Griffiths took part – all of them having ridden motor-cycles in 1910, except of course 'H.F.S.' with his Morgan Runabout. In deference to the advancing years, all opted for four wheels in 1935 – except 'H.F.S.' and George Brough who were loyal to their old forms of transport.

While the *Exeter* was quickly growing in toughness and repute as a trial, the *Land's End*, too, was 'developing'. To appease the public, prizes had been awarded for many years in the motor-cycle classes for the most silent machine. In the 1934 *Land's End* Masters invited the car entry to compete, and a Ford V8 took the prize. Keeping the severity of the observed sections abreast of the

1939: Though some of the cars are beginning to look more like those of today, the horse was still very much in evidence on MCC hills. This one waits patiently near the summit of an observed section, ready to haul up the failures.

1934: A Wolseley Hornet awaits its turn to climb Beggars' Roost in the Land's End Trial. Though never as successful as their direct rivals the MG Midgets, these small six-cylinder sports cars were popular in racing events.

1934: One way up Beggars' Roost! This MG is helped to the summit by the hard-working team of marshals with a tow-rope, and the ever-helpful St John's Ambulance Brigade.

increasing capabilities of competing vehicles, he moved the Beggars' Roost start line 20 yards farther up the hill – and 103 competitors failed to get away; Barton Steep, Hustyn and Darracott accounted for 154 failures between them, with roughly equal numbers on each hill.

No story of the MCC classic trials would be complete without brief mention of the various MG teams, which were to become perhaps the best known of all trials teams during the thirties – it is a story that would almost fill a book. The original J2 Midgets of the earlier MG team were replaced in 1934 by PA Midgets (Toulmin, Crawford and Jones), becoming the famous 'Cream Cracker' team in 1935. These were followed successively by the supercharged PB Midgets in 1936, the TA Midgets in 1937, and the TAs of 1938, fitted with $1^{1}/_{2}$-litre VA engines enlarged to 1,700cc – all running as 'Cream Crackers'. It is the first 'Cream Cracker' team that concerns us here, which ran in the December 1935 *Exeter* alongside another MG team, the 'Three Musketeers' (Archie Langley, Bastock and Macdermid).

The 'Musketeers' had originated during the early part of 1935, consisting of three of the six MG NE Magnettes that had run in the 1934 Ulster Tourist Trophy race; only seven were built, and Dodson won the race in one of them.

Fitted with more suitable bodywork, the three 'Musketeer' trials cars were named *Athos*, *Porthos* and *Aramis* – the first two driven by MG Company employees F. Kindell and S. Nash, and the third by L. Welsh. They made their trials debut in the 1935 *Land's End*, winning three Premier Awards, and followed this up by winning three more PAs in the *Edinburgh*. In July that year they added further glory to their record when they won the team prize in the MCC Welsh Rally – Nash winning the event outright in *Aramis*, the car in which Dodson had won the previous year's TT!

When the MG Company closed their racing department in mid-1935, the splendid NE Magnettes were sold to Kenneth and Denis Evans' Bellevue Garage and, restored to their racing trim, ran in the 1935 TT. The three 'Musketeers' themselves turned to PA-Type Midgets – named, of course, *Athos*, *Porthos* and *Aramis* – for the MCC's Torquay Rally; and these cars, too, had a history having run as George Eyston's 'Dancing Daughters' team in the 1935 Le Mans 24-hours.

A trio of curiously hybrid, but extremely potent Magnettes formed the new 'Three Musketeers' team for events in 1935–6, built up with selected parts from a variety of MG models and all three supercharged. It was this

1939: Harbinger of a day when family saloons would outnumber sports cars, R. Truscott's ordinary-looking Talbot saloon prepares to climb Crackington in the *Land's End* – his number, 446, indicating the vast size of the entry that year.

1939: Dick Shattock (famous for his RGS Atalanta racing-sports cars post-World War II) attempts the Darracott re-start in his Austin Seven. He was another to cut his teeth in MCC events before making a name for himself in motor racing.

team that joined the 'Cream Crackers' at the start of the 1935 *Exeter* – and one can understand the feelings of the many drivers in privately-entered teams when these two tied for the team prize with identical performances! And what better evidence could there be of the versatility of the NE Magnette than a win in the Tourist Trophy, followed by an outstandingly successful year in trials, including an outright win and team prize in a rally – and then back to the TT again?

These weren't the only teams of course. There were the little green supercharged Austin Sevens of the 'Grasshopper' team (D. Buckley, H. L. Hadley and W. H. Scriven); and the curiously named 'Candidi Provocatores' team of Singers (Baker, Barnes and A. H. Langley) – which we took to mean 'White Challengers' because the cars were white. And the 'Tailwaggers' team of Allard Specials – which sprang from Sidney Allard's first Allard Special trials car (as distinct from his four-wheeled Morgan three-wheeler) with its Grand Prix Bugatti body. It was fashionable then to build trials specials around the 30hp Ford V8 – before the post-war era of lightweight Ford 1,172cc-engined, 'sporting trial' cars.

The choice of three starting points was introduced for the 1935 *Edinburgh* (Carlisle, Stratford-on-Avon and Wrotham Park), for the *Land's End* in 1936

(Virginia Water, Stratford-on-Avon and Penzance), and for the *Exeter* in 1937 (Stratford-on-Avon, Virginia Water and Penzance). This latest of Masters' innovations made no difference to the total mileage covered between start and finish – which, in each event, was more or less the same whichever starting point was chosen. It did, however, considerably reduce the 'wasted' mileage covered by some people in getting to the original London starts. The old titles, London-Exeter, London-Land's End and London-Edinburgh became something of a misnomer, though they were retained.

At this time there was a section of the Committee who felt that the night runs to the points at which the testing nature of the trials began had become redundant – they had no influence on the results now that the unreliability bugbear had been completely overcome. However, it was felt then, as it is now, that they were what gave the MCC events their unique character, and that to drop them would break the continuity. But the subject comes up from time to time, even today.

In a sense this brings up the old problem of 'suitable for everyday vehicles'. As things are, the night runs demand lighting equipment, and at least a degree of refinement (although some of today's entries provide little more protection than a surfboard); and the scrutineers at the start demand complete compli-

1939: Running as a member of the three-car 'Musketeers' team of MG Magnettes, J. A. Bastock puts paid to the idea that the ban on 'knobblies' would ruin the sport – by rocketing up Darracott in the Land's End Trial.

1939: Another famous MG driver, Maurice Toulmin (usually in the three-car 'Cream Crackers' team of MG Midgets), turned out for the *Land's End* in a four-seater N-Type Magnette – seen here 'jumping-the-gun' at a timed re-start!

ance with the Road Traffic Act. If the trials were to degenerate into one-day events, held in daylight, there would be no need for full road equipment, and the vehicles could become out-and-out trials specials, demanding far tougher sections – with the complete exclusion of 'everyday vehicles' and a total change in character of these historic events. Let us hope the Committee will never be so misguided as to make this change.

For many years the *Exeter* had been held on the Friday night and Saturday following Christmas Day – and this put the 1936 event forward to 1 and 2 January 1937. Windout and Pin hills were introduced and proved easy – though not for the Chairman and Secretary who, during a route inspection, had spent a couple hours searching for a farmer with a couple of horses to extricate their Riley from Windout. Simms, running true to form, stopped 106 entries, but Fingle only 29. Among the big – huge, even – cars were a Speed Six Bentley, 3-litre Sunbeam, 4,620cc Packard, two 3,679cc Lammas-Grahams, 3-litre Invicta, $2^{1}/_{2}$-litre Daimler, 3,358cc Chevrolet and a 3-litre Talbot 105.

The 1937 *Exeter* was held on 7 and 8 January 1938 – historians please note these anomalies! Hills included Windout, Fingle, Simms, Higher Rill, Woodhaynes and Knowle Lane (both near Bridport), with the finish moved to the Grand Hotel, Bournemouth. Fingle —divided into two sections — stopped 63, and Simms only 52 ('Simms is not what it used to be ', wrote one reporter, with truth). Out of 180 car entries, 84 claimed Premier Awards. The final pre-war *Exeter* was held on 6 and 7 January 1939, being notable for the large number of 'official' Army motor-cycle entries — as had been the *Land's End* for several years. This Army participation in MCC trials had been recommended by the War Office 'because of the excellent training value' — and this year, for the first time, the Army riders on their standard road tyres ran on equal terms with the rest of the entries because the RAC had placed a ban on 'knobblies' (competition tyres). Their deep, spiky treads carried too much mud on to the main roads. As a result of the Army's interest, for the first time for many years the motor-cycle entry in the *Exeter* exceeded the cars, at 205 to 151, 69 of the motor-cycles being Army-entered.

Despite Simms not having been what it was in 1938, Masters made it optional for Premier Awards, with special prizes for 'clean' climbs — of which 66 were claimed. This was the final event in the last pre-war Annual Team

1938: Almost in sight of the *Land's End* finish — F. Harris fell asleep and his F-Super Morgan hit a wall. In the centre of the group of mourners is author Peter Garnier who arrived on the scene in his own JAP-engined Super Sports.

1937: Phil Uglow, one of the earliest customers for an HRG sports car – a newcomer which had made its MCC debut in the 1936 *Land's End* – is seen tackling Darracott. This car still competes in Westcountry trials, driven by Phil's son, David Uglow.

Championship, awarded for the best performance by a team of the same three cars in the yearly series of MCC trials. It was won – predictably – by the $1^{1}/_{2}$-litre 'Cream Cracker' MG TA Midgets driven by J. M. Toulmin, H. K. Crawford and J. E. S. Jones.

By the time of the 1936 *Land's End* the MCC had added road-building to their role of road-repairer, having achieved their long-held ambition to obtain a lease on Bluehills Mine, near Newquay, where the old hill was becoming too easy (it is tarred now, and in daily use). By the 1936 trial their excavations had resulted in a straight, extremely stony 1 in 3 climb with a precipitous drop down to the sea on its right-hand side. Of the 518 entries (327 of them cars) this new, private hill stopped only 20, being approached by a relatively level stretch on which speed could be built up for the main assault. It was clear that sooner or later at least one – and probably more – of these flat-out exponents was going to mount the low parapet and vanish down the precipice into the sea.

To prevent this, further extensive excavations were undertaken before the 1937 event, by-passing the straight run-in with very tight, left-right hairpins, the latter precipitously steep with rock outcrops that are extremely slippery when wet, and a big hump at the apex. To make doubly sure, they laid a 12-yard patch of solid concrete on the steepest part, near the summit, where a stop-and-restart test was introduced. This did the trick in what was reported as 'The Toughest Land's End For Many Years'. Out of 276 cars entered, Bluehills stopped 178; and only 20 Premier Awards were claimed. As will be seen later, as motor-cycle and car performances improved, so did the speeds up Bluehills, with the dangers of a drop down the precipice returning – although it has always been heavily guarded by sandbags. Even more extensive earth- and rock-shifting was to be undertaken in the eighties.

Extending over 180 miles of road, the huge 459-strong cavalcade in the 1939 *Land's End* (including 247 motor-cycles) took six full hours to pass – from the first motor-cycle to the final car. The breakfast halt, as had been traditional for many years, was at Deller's Cafe, near Taunton, the converging point of the three overnight routes. And, in their reports of the event (*The Motor Cycle*'s occupied five pages), the journalists were unanimously impressed by the huge crowds gathered at the observed sections – even at 3am on Doverhay, first of the hills and one which was climbed only by the motor-cycle entry; at Bluehills the sides of the valley were black with people, as someone put it 'like roosting starlings'.

1937: Dickie Green, one of the multitude of MG Midget campaigners who dominated the entry lists of MCC trials during the 1930s, climbs New Mill in the Land's End Trial.

1939: As a young man, the author cut his pre-war competition teeth with a 1,096cc JAP-engined Super Sports Morgan (seen here on Barton Steep in the *Land's End*) – the second of three much-loved Morgan 'trikes'.

A fine hare, lashed to the back of K. S. Fishers's Ariel Square-Four sidecar outfit – a trophy killed somewhere along the route – brought loud cheers from the spectators. Bluehills again played its part as the MCC's principal stopper, though, as *The Motor Cycle* recorded, the newly imposed ban on 'knobbly' tyres seemed to affect performances very little, but the wear-and-tear on ordinary road tyres was considerable and costly. The MCC Film Unit, under the direction of J. C. Lowe, managed to show a first-class film of the event at the Club's Easter Sunday dinner at Exeter – 122 miles from the finish and fewer than twenty-four hours after it. This last pre-World War II *Land's End* was the twenty-seventh in the series, and of the large, 229-strong contingent of motor-cycles and three-wheelers that actually started in the event, 188 completed the course, 55 claiming Premier Awards, 58 Silver Medals and 65 Bronze. Of the 212 car entries, 64 claimed PAs – Bluehills alone having accounted for 95 failures (97 cars in 1938, when the car entry claimed 68 PAs).

Concerned that the Scottish section of the *Edinburgh* was providing little entertainment for spectators and few challenges to competitors, Jackie Masters started searching for new observed hills north of the Border, and came up with Costerton and Humble hills in the Lauder area for the 1937 event. Despite the ban on locked axles, imposed for the 1936 *Edinburgh* and subsequent MCC trials, these proved easy though 'interesting', stopping only twenty-seven competitors between them. In the reports it was described as the 'Easiest *Edinburgh* for years', with 142 starters, 96 of whom claimed Premier Awards. The following year, 1938, the Scottish Sporting Car Club came to the rescue and unearthed two real stoppers – Adderstonshiels and Gattonside, which proved to be just what the Club wanted. Between them they brought 107 competitors to a standstill and the 1938 *Edinburgh* went into the records book with only thirty-four PAs – the lowest number ever awarded in this traditionally easy event.

One further new hill appeared in the route cards for the 29 May 1939 trial, final pre-World War II *Edinburgh*. Named Blackford, it was situated in the public gardens right in the City and within sight of the final check-point at the top of the hill. A stop-and-restart test made things more difficult, and added interest for the many spectators, putting paid to Premier Awards for nineteen competitors with otherwise clean sheets. The MCC Film Unit, ever on the ball, put on a technicolour recording of the trial at a memorable luncheon at the Black Barony Hotel in Peebles on Whit Sunday, the day following the finish.

At the outbreak of war, membership was strong – thanks to a large extent to the interest shown by the Army in using the MCC trials as a training exercise. Out of the seventy-six new motor-cycle members listed on

14 December 1938, sixty-two held commissioned or non-commissioned ranks in the Army, thirteen of them in the City of London Signals. This influx of Army riders continued through 1939, with fifteen more joining the Club in February.

CHAPTER 5

At War Again

It is interesting to recall, nearly fifty years later, the reluctance of human nature to accept change, and how optimistically we all carried on with our normal lives when the sky was heavily overcast with the black clouds of war. The Minutes of the 23 August 1939 Committee meeting make no mention of the uncertainty ahead. The dates for the 1940 calendar of events were drawn up: Land's End Trial (22 and 23 March), Edinburgh Trial (10 and 11 May), Inter-Club Team Trial (1 June), Harrogate Rally (4–6 June), Donington Meeting (27 July), Brooklands Meeting (7 September), and Exeter Trial (3 and 4 January 1941). Applications were made to the ACU for confirmation of these dates at their forthcoming meeting on 22 September. For the *Exeter* it was planned to use the following hills: Windout, Fingle (motor-cycles and sidecar outfits only), Simms, Strete's, Harcombe, Meerhay, Ryall (solos only), Woodhaye, Beacon Hill (if found suitable) and a new hill near Wareham.

At this same meeting, no fewer than twenty-one applications for membership were accepted – including, as I see now, one or two close motor-cycling friends who were soon to lose their lives in World War II.

At the 15 September meeting, with the 'phoney war' already twelve days old, it was minuted: 'In view of the present conditions, it was decided that the Club should close down all its activities for the time being, and that if possible the offices (at 1 Queen Victoria Street, London EC4) should be sub-let.' It was agreed that suspension of membership subscriptions should be announced in the technical press.

So far as the Club's finances were concerned, during the close-down for World War II, the 9 September Brooklands meeting had been cancelled with a greatly oversubscribed entry list, and entry fees were returned to members less 25 per cent (practically all the expenses of organisation having been incurred before the meeting had been cancelled). On 15 September a resolution was passed, allowing the Treasurer to sell such stock as was necessary to provide the Club with the ready money required to keep going; and, in view of his sudden loss of income, it was agreed to give the Secretary a cheque for £100 to continue his services until the end of 1939.

The Secretary's financial position was further discussed on 5 January 1940 when a letter from him was read to the Committee in respect of his expenditure on office rent and clerical assistance during the six years prior to the Club's taking over their present office in Bloomsbury. It was minuted: 'The Committee decided they did not wish to discuss the details of the letter but were prepared to discuss the future position of the Secretary . . .'. They agreed to pay him a retaining fee of £104 per year as from 25 September 1939, subject to revision from time to time – with which, it is recorded, the Secretary was delighted. It was a wise decision, for the Secretary at the time, and for many years afterwards, was Jackie Masters (see Chapter 12), one of the all-time 'greats' of the MCC. At the same meeting the Treasurer was authorised to sell '. . .up to £200 nominal of the Club's holding of India $4^{1}/_{2}$ per cent Stock 1950/1955'.

Predictably, at the 9 January 1940 meeting it was reported that the ACU were unlikely to hold their 1940 date-fixing conference. All members who had paid their 1939 subscriptions were to be retained on the Membership Register until such time as they were required to pay a further subscription; and a date for the 1940 AGM was fixed for 15 March – no fewer than 36 members turning up.

Peter Clark suggested that the Committee might explore the possibility of holding trials of a simple nature during the war. Messrs Toomey, Mayne, Kelshaw, Freeman, Porter, Marians and Roundhill took part in the discussion, Bob Porter suggesting the possible use of alternative fuels. The Chairman pointed out that, although the RAC had just decided that no permits should be granted for motor-car trials during the war, the same decision had not been taken by the ACU regarding motor-cycle events. How unwilling we were to abandon the old ways! More practicable, though, Major Marians proposed that social events should continue – not cheap affairs (a maximum charge of 5/- for dinner was suggested) but that, for a start, 'a really good evening should be the aim'. This suggestion was accepted unanimously – a trifle ingenuously, in view of rationing – and Major Marians was given the task of setting it up. Nothing, however, seems to have come of it.

The monthly Committee meetings continued bravely through 1940 and up to April 1941, the Committee now consisting of older members – or those still too young to join the Forces – though many of those already serving continued to attend during their leaves. Such names appear regularly on the attendance lists as Arthur Bourne (editor of *The Motor Cycle*), Major Marians (Club Captain), Peter Clark (well-known BRDC member), Bob Porter, E. C. Lumiss, Jackie Masters (Secretary), Leslie Freeman, Harold Hastings (*The Motor*), J. C. Lowe, L. A. Baddeley, H. M. Toomey (who, together with J. F. Whitfield, rode immaculately prepared BMWs in pre-war MCC trials), T. N. Blockley (later a member of the Rootes Group international rally team), Denis Jenkinson (then working at the Royal Aircraft Establishment, Farnborough) and others well-known before and after the war.

During 1942 only the AGM was held (on 7 May, the 1 Queen Victoria Street registered offices still being used) and a Committee meeting on 30 July, the principal subject for discussion being news of the activities of members serving in HM Forces. Even during those tense years, when the future was less predictable even than the weather, applications for membership were still being received. At the 10 March 1943 meeting the Executive accepted more than a dozen such applications for immediate membership – which were accepted at the usual subscription rates, to cover the period until the first active post-war season. Still the subject of social gatherings cropped up, and arrangements were made with the Waldorf Hotel in London's Aldwych for a get-together on 14 May 1943, the 'good running buffet' to cost 6/6d per head ($32^1/_2$p by today's reckoning). Notices of this function were sent to all traceable members. Further Committee meetings were held during 1943 on 31 July and 20 October.

The on-going matter of ACU affiliation (and by now, RAC too) which had punctuated the MCC's affairs since the early days came up for discussion once more. A confidential report, issued to all Committee members, is worth quoting in full for it contains historical information about the thinking on such matters:

In accordance with the decision of the Committee at their meeting on 21 July 1943 that the question of the Club affiliating with the RAC and ACU be explored, the Chairman and the Secretary had a preliminary discussion with Captain A. W. Phillips of the RAC on 7 September 1943.

The benefits of Associated membership of the RAC are given in the enclosed booklets. These benefits can be obtained by joining the RAC direct, or by becoming a member of an Associated Club. By joining such a club a considerable reduction in the RAC subscription is obtained. There are at present over 80 clubs in the RAC scheme, including – with one or two exceptions – every motor club of note.

From the MCC point of view, the advantage of being an Association Club would be that it could offer an added inducement to people to join, particularly the large number who, although very interested in the sporting side of motoring, do not wish to compete in trials. The Club already has a long list of such people who give great assistance in the organisation of the Club's events, act as officials, and like to be kept in touch with the Club's affairs. At the same time there is no point in these people becoming members and paying a subscription, although in many cases they actually do so. If the Club could offer them RAC benefits, *including* all MCC benefits for the same amount of subscription that it would cost them to join the RAC direct (and this should be possible), there is no doubt that the MCC would get an increased and influential membership.

It should be borne in mind that the scheme applies to both motor-cycle and car owners. The RAC motor-cycle associate membership is entirely distinct from ACU motor-cycle affiliation; the latter does not include any touring benefits.

The possibility that the Club's normal activities may be restricted by legislation should not be overlooked; and should it become necessary to consider any reorganisation it would be useful to have some inducement such as RAC Associate Membership to offer our members whilst fresh plans are being made.

The Club has always had very cordial relations with the RAC and it is understood that the latter would welcome an approach from the MCC for Associate Membership as being a step in the best interests of the sport in general.

The question of affiliation to the ACU is a little more complex owing to the constitution of that body. It is understood, however, that an approach by the MCC would be cordially welcomed.

The present position is that, as the result of prolonged negotiations in 1926, an agreement between the MCC and ACU was signed whereby the MCC undertook to recognise the ACU as the controlling body for motor-cycle sport and to abide by its rules and regulations; and the ACU accepted the MCC as 'an approved, non-constituent club' without any representation on the ACU Council or Committee.

This arrangement has worked quite satisfactorily as a whole, principally because the MCC has had no desire to take any part in the control of the sport. The agreement has, however, been the subject of adverse comment by newcomers to the ACU Council from time to time, on the grounds that it is illogical to give favourable treatment to an unaffiliated club.

The general framework of the ACU is such that a club affiliates to its local Centre of the ACU, this Centre controlling affairs in its own area. Delegates are appointed by each Centre to the ACU Council, which is the governing body. The Council elects the various committees (Management, Competition, etc.) annually. There is, however, a section for Non-Territorial Clubs, who do not belong to a local Centre but affiliate direct to the ACU. The MCC would come under this heading with direct representation on the Council by the maximum number of club delegates (viz. three).

Although the ACU rules provide for the inclusion of all members in an affiliation scheme, it is understood that a proposal to affiliate the motor-cycle members of the MCC as a Non-Territorial Club would be accepted.

The principal advantages accruing to the MCC would be that, as an affiliated club, it would retain as a right everything it now gets under an agreement (and would thus remove the cause of such anti-MCC feeling as exists); and we would, furthermore, have direct representation by three delegates on the ACU Council, with an opportunity of representation on the various committees.

The affiliation of the MCC would enormously strengthen the ACU, and it may happen that post-war legislation may make it very desirable that the MCC, in its own interests, should be in a position to take a prominent part in any negotiations that may become necessary to prevent restrictive legislation from being put into force.

The Committee received this report at the 20 October 1943 meeting and it was agreed that, if Associate Membership of the RAC would not entail raising the normal MCC subscription and that it need be taken up only by those wishing to do so, there was no objection. As ever, though, the Committee were highly suspicious of ACU affiliation and whatever it might entail — agreeing that, although there was probably 'something to be said for it in post-war conditions', very careful consideration would have to be given to safeguarding the Club's interests. The general body of members, they felt, would have to be consulted before a decision could be taken, and a sub-committee was set up to investigate the matter.

This sensitive cauldron bubbled on . . . and on, while the sub-committee had regular talks and lengthy correspondence with the RAC and ACU, reporting back to the main Committee at successive meetings. It was not until 25 January 1945 that agreement was reached with the RAC that the capitation fee should be 15/- a year for motor-cycle Associate Membership and £1 for cars — to which the Committee gave its blessing. And, on 20 February 1946 agreement was reached to make formal application for affiliation with the ACU, after some 40 years of doubt and misgiving.

With hopes rising of a return to normal, meetings were stepped-up to every second month in 1945. In May 1945, with petrol rationing still very much in force, it was decided to run an informal rally at Wrotham Park, the date being fixed for 3 July. There was nothing competitive about this, simply a gathering of like-minded people, but it was an unqualified success, turning out to be Britain's first post-war 'motoring event'. It indicated the almost irrepressible enthusiasm for motoring that had lain dormant throughout the war years. Despite more pressing demands on their meagre fuel supplies, 100 or so cars and 12 motor-cycles turned up, many old members travelling considerable distances; several prospective members also came along to join.

Application was made on 18 July 1945 for renewal of the lease of the MCC's offices at 26 Bloomsbury Way, London, at an annual rent of £90, exclusive of rates and taxes; and, in view of the shortage of funds after the non-productive war years, subscriptions were raised to £2 and £1 respectively for cars and motor-cycles, with a 10/- entry fee in each case. The possibility of holding an abbreviated Exeter Trial in January 1946 was discussed. Applications for membership came pouring in, including such well-known drivers as Ken Hutchison, George Abecassis, E. J. Newton (of HRG fame), Ian Baillie, Ken Burgess, A. R. Mallock, Raymond Way and many others.

Most significant perhaps was that the long-delayed admission of women members to the MCC was proposed at the 1946 AGM (26 January) by L. G. Eckett, and seconded by A. F. Scroggs, well-known Trojan campaigner in MCC trials, and carried by 25 votes to five.

Plans were drawn up for a full sporting programme in 1946, including the *Exeter*, *Land's End* and *Edinburgh* trials (January, April and June respectively), Inter-Club Motor-cycle Trial (July), Speed Events (July and September – though this was to become a problem, Brooklands having gone and Donington still occupied by the Army), Sporting Trial (October) and, for 1947, the Exeter Trial in January. The form (or even the holding) of these depended of course on the extent, or even the complete lifting, of the petrol ration.

In high hopes of running the *Exeter* in 1946, the Chairman, L. A. Baddeley, reported at the October 1945 meeting that he had spent four days covering the entire 1939 route. All the old familiar hills were in 'very good trials condition' – Fingle, Simms, Windout, Harcombe, Woodhayes, Higher Rill and Meerhay; as an alternative to Higher Rill, Swains Hill had been 'discovered'. Local authorities along the route gave their wholehearted blessing to the resumption of the MCC 'clas,ics' – Deller's Cafe at Exeter, traditional breakfast stop on the Exeter Trial, and a host of others, including the Lynton and Lynmouth Electric Light Company who particularly wanted to know when the *Land's End* would be held. They needed to estimate their electricity requirements because the large number of visitors attracted by the trial considerably increased the electricity demand.

At the same meetintg L. A. Baddeley, who also held the post of Treasurer, 'intimated his desire to relinquish the post' – having held it since January 1911!

The Committee were faced by a formidable task – planning a full-scale *Exeter* for January 1946 on the reasonable enough assumption that British motorists would have ration-free petrol (as had already been the case with our American allies for some time) and, at the same time, preparing for an abbreviated event if restrictions were still in force. Tentative announcements were made to the technical Press, which at least indicated to members that their committee had their interests at heart though, at the March 1946 meeting – by which time no *Exeter* had been held – they were compelled to postpone the *Edinburgh* and *Land's End* too, and to announce the postponement of all long-distance trials.

At least they were able to agree that, in view of the tyre shortage, 'knobbly' competition tyres – banned in 1939 – would be admitted for the time being, subject to RAC approval. Cars were not all that plentiful either, with many special-purpose ex-WD vehicles in private use. It was necessary to re-draft the definition of vehicles eligible to compete in MCC trials. The principal requirement remained that only private passenger vehicles were eligible, and that four-wheel-drive and Service vehicles of all types were banned – with the exception of Staff saloon and touring cars, and utility cars with utility bodywork mounted on ordinary private passenger car chassis.

The general MCC trials regulations were re-drafted and divided into two headings: standard regulations applicable to all trials and issued to members at the start of each season; and regulations applicable to individual trials, to be included in the appropriate prospectus.

An attempt was made to run a Midland Rally in July of 1946, with tests for motor-cycles and cars in a 48-acre field belonging to the George Hotel at Shipston-on-Stour. Regulations were drawn up and a prospectus sent out to members, but the number of entries did not reach the seventy-five minimum set by the Committee. It was decided to run it as an 'assembly', similar to the gathering in Wrotham Park that had heralded the return to peacetime 'fun' motoring. The gathering of vehicles was not impressive, but more than one hundred members and guests attended the dinner-and-dance at the George, where practically the entire hotel was put at the disposal of the Club by the proprietor, Mr Whitter, himself an old MCC member.

The year 1946 was not all disappointment, however. The Inter-Club Team Trial (now sub-titled the Championship of the Clubs - see Chapter 10) was held successfully on War Department land in the Aldershot area with twenty-four teams of six motor-cycles taking part. There would have been twenty-five teams, but the Birmingham MCC 'lost' one of their machines in transit, and did not take part. In reply to their request for a refund of their entry fee it was explained to them that they could, as one or two other teams had done successfully, have competed with only five riders.

The Sporting Trial, too, was held, using the old 1938 route in the Buxton area on 2 November; as the result of a questionnaire sent to members, forty-nine car owners and twenty-six motor-cyclists agreed to take part, along with forty who volunteered as officials. Undeterred even by rationing, it appears that by now competitors were having their vehicles transported to the scene of action — for a Mr Roberts put in a claim for £10 to repair damage to a wall by Messrs Pickford's removal van, which at the time had been operating in the MCC's interests.

A return to the three classic trials was obviously being given high priority, though it was announced in the Sporting Trial programme that it was unlikely the *Exeter* would be held on the proposed dates of 3 and 4 January 1947. Arthur Bourne suggested that it would be possible to organise a full-scale *Exeter*, even on the existing fuel ration, if limited to motor-cycles, but this was turned down on the grounds that it would be wrong to revive the long-awaited classics with a motor-cycles-only event.

So far as the *Land's End* was concerned, it was decided in December 1946 to run the event next year, regardless of any possible increase in the fuel ration. An abbreviated event, starting at Taunton and finishing at Bluehills Mine, near Newquay and following the old 1939 route was decided upon – a distance of 200 miles. No fewer than 293 members entered – 103 solo motor-cycles, 28 sidecars, 2 three-wheelers and 160 cars. But, as if punishing competitors for that old wartime crime of 'the mis-use of petrol', the weather was appalling. Not all the car entry had the opportunity of passing through the New Mill and Bluehills Mine sections, due to the delays caused, so these sections had to be omitted from the car entry when calculating the results.

On the return journey to Malvern Link, Peter Morgan was stopped in Launceston for exceeding the speed limit, a misdemeanour for which he was subsequently summonsed and fined. With commendable honesty he confessed to the Stewards, who regretfully told him they had no option but to withdraw his Premier Award.

Though there were strong misgivings among Committee members as to the wisdom of running another lengthy event so soon after the *Land's End*, arrangements went ahead for the 1947 *Edinburgh* at Whitsun, in modified form and centred on Harrogate. Again the entry was strong with 38 solos, 6 sidecars, 1 three-wheeler and 81 cars. In their report of the event, the Stewards summed up the four observed hills used in the trial, all relics from pre-war days: 'Middle Tongue – hardly worth keeping unless it rains. Park Rash – still a satisfactory hill. Summer Lodge – still the best hill of the trial. Bouthwaite – possibly all right if it rains; not very interesting.' One of the comments made was that a 'social organiser' would help new members to feel more 'a part of the family' at the hotel in the evening, again emphasising the strong family atmosphere at MCC events.

The first long-distance motor-cycle races post-war had been the Junior and Senior Manx Grands Prix in September of 1946, run on low-octane Pool petrol – as of course had been all other sporting events; and they were to continue to do so for some time to come. Even reduced compression ratios and larger jet sizes did not prevent endless trouble with burned exhaust valves, and the increased fuel consumption that resulted from these de-tuning measures. The same applied to the Senior TT, held in June 1946. For the motor-racing fraternity, the first brief enjoyment of the sport had been in a speed trial on 28 October 1945, run by the resourceful Bristol club on the Filton Aerodrome runway.

As an indication of the burgeoning enthusiasm for motor sport at the time, ninety-four new members were elected to the MCC in February-March 1947 – 38 motor-cycles, 45 cars and a single three-wheeler. We lived in perpetual hope of a sudden change in the policy of a government that had promised so much, including 'fair shares for all'. The only snag about the shares was that they were parsimonious beyond words with fuel shortages, power shortages, food shortages and the rest – and, above all, no 'fun' motoring. The position was not made any more acceptable by the fact that the French, whose country had been enemy-occupied almost throughout the conflict, had run a successful motor-race meeting in the Bois de Boulogne in September 1945. Though we never knew what changes there might be in the basic ration from month to month, somehow we were getting by. The Team Trial for motor-cycles was held on War Department land near Liphook in 1947 and, later in the year, the mixed-entry Sporting Trial with headquarters at the Palace Hotel, Buxton, and an entry totalling ninety-five, compared with seventy-six in 1946. By now MCC membership stood at 360 cars and 230 motor-cycles.

The basic petrol ration, as distinct from the continuing wartime allowance for essential motoring, had been restored in June 1945, allowing 150 miles of non-essential motoring each month. In March 1946 this had been increased to allow 180 miles a month, and again in August 1946 to allow 260. But in October 1947 even this meagre concession for 'pleasure' motoring came abruptly to an end. Once again, only those who could prove an essential need for personal transport were permitted to use their cars. There were protest meetings and petitions galore; one of these presented to the government was said to contain more than two million signatures. But to no avail and it was not until eight non-motoring months had passed that the basic allowance was restored in June 1948 with 90 miles a month, or 1,080 a year, compared with the average pre-war annual mileage of 7,000 by private motorists. It was doubled to 180 during the summer of 1949 and petrol rationing came finally and riotously to an end in May 1950.

Apart from having to return to social gatherings during this second period of sporting inactivity, the Committee applied themselves to the future policy and activities of the Club, the sub-committee's lengthy report containing eighty-three items for consideration. Since the income had not met expenditure since well before the war, finance was high on the list, and the broad policy was to attract more members, comparisons being made with the Vintage Sports Car Club, MG Car Club and Junior Car Club (later BARC) which then stood at 1,000, 800 and 2,500 respectively. Various methods of achieving this were discussed, including extensive advertising aimed especially at the younger generation who, because of the war, knew nothing of the pleasures of membership and the Club's several classic events. Special note was taken of the attendance in 1948 at the first post-war Motor Show, which had exceeded two million, more than twice that of the pre-war record figure. This, they felt, could be taken as a strong indication of the great upsurge of interest in cars – and its potential in attracting new members.

The reintroduction of the *Gazette* was recommended (later to be published as *Triple*); bulk insurance for cars and motor-cycles, local Centres (as with the ACU), each competing for an Inter-Centre award, and many other matters were discussed. Special emphasis was made on the encouragement of standard production cars and motor-cycles in all but the most sporting events; and a Novice's Award was recommended for those who had not yet won a 'Gold' in any of the Club's events. The setting up of a permanent road circuit was regarded as important, particularly since a 110-acre site was available at £30-£50 an acre; presumably the proposers of this idea had the BRDC's Silverstone and the BARC's Goodwood, both opened in 1948, in mind.

Many of these proposals were turned down by the main committee, but the need for increased membership, and the achievement of it by extensive advertising, were agreed. No changes were felt necessary in the type or number of events; and it was optimistically agreed that, when petrol became freely available, the Club would be 'swamped with entries for all the classic trials'. It was, in brief, a policy of maintaining the status quo until the effects of readily available, graded petrol could be assessed.

With the return of the basic ration, the Sporting and Inter-Club Team trials were held in the latter months of 1948. An abbreviated, 54-mile *Exeter* was held in January 1949, the Committee going to considerable trouble to investigate road and rail transport to carry competing motor-cycles and cars from London to Exeter. An entry of 90 was received – 31 solos, 4 sidecars, 2 three-wheelers and 53 cars. The *Land's End*, too, was run using a circular 60-mile route starting and finishing at Lynton, based on the Devon Trial route. At 159, the entry was strong with 58 solos, 14 sidecars, 2 three-wheelers and 85 cars. The *Edinburgh*, at Whitsun, kept to the austerity route based on Harrogate. New events included the Minehead Rally, held in September with a few driving tests and two hill-climbs; and, as a complete innovation, a Continental Run which attracted twelve cars and a sidecar, the event being reported as an outstanding success and a sphere of MCC activity which should be expanded. The Sporting and Inter-Club trials were held as usual late in the year – and the Committee took the bold step of booking the Silverstone circuit for the Club's first post-war race meeting, to be held on 9 September 1950. It was also decided to run two Continental sorties in 1950, one to Barcelona (subsequently cancelled through lack of entries) and the other to Lugano.

The 1950 *Exeter* was held on 31 December 1949 so that, for the first time in the Club's history, there were two *Exeters* in one year. The *Land's End* stuck to its traditional Easter date — and the by now almost traditional route from Taunton to Bluehills Mine — with the Lynton and Lynmouth Council presenting a special trophy in recognition of the trade which the event brought to the towns. It is engraved 'The Lyn Trophy Presented by the Townspeople of Lynton and Lynmouth'. For a change, the *Edinburgh* (which had at one time been in danger of postponement until a full-scale event could again be held) became a night trial, covering 100 miles and including Middle Tongue, Park Rash and three new observed sections. A month later petrol rationing came to an end.

Looking back over those lean wartime years one cannot but marvel at the stamina and sustained optimism of the Committee in keeping things going without a break. And when peacetime returned, with its meagre on-off petrol allowances, there was no resentment at the cut-down form the classic trials were forced to take — only joy that they were being held at all, despite some feelings of guilt that, one way or another, we were managing to cover in competitive events more miles than ever the Ministry of Fuel and Power had provided for with their wretched coupons.

CHAPTER 6

Second Re-start

Despite the heavy work-load involved in preparing for a return to normal in June, the Committee found time to attend to several significant matters during the early part of 1950. Mrs Lord, who, as Miss Muriel Hind, had achieved so many successes on two, three and four wheels in the very early days of the Club, was elected an honorary life member. The Committee were told that 'as one of the original lady members she had joined in 1905 and had continued her membership unbroken right up to date'. Yet it was not until January 1946 that the decision was taken to admit lady members – a curious anomaly.

Whether the Club should change its name came up for discussion, as it had done in the past and was to do for many years to come. With the preponderance of car-owning membership, and with the possibility of future car members being deterred from joining a 'motor-cycling club', it was felt that a change was probably overdue. This was raised at the 1950 AGM, and although the Committee were almost wholly in agreement, the members voted against it. In anticipation of the Club's Golden Jubilee in 1951, a year it shared with the Festival of Britain, the possibility of producing an 'MCC Jubilee Book' covering the first fifty years of the Club's long history was discussed – and heartily approved. That great motoring historian Dudley Noble was suggested as the author and he was brought into subsequent discussions, but the idea was dropped – presumably because of the immense amount of research involved (and, let it be said, the surprising lack of any official records, a problem faced throughout the compiling of this book!).

At the time, with so many clubs wanting to hire the Silverstone circuit for speed events, it was decided to form a Silverstone Supporter's Club, of which a meeting was held at the RAC in April – the MCC contributing £10 towards the funds. Successful race meetings were held on the circuit, notably by the Aston Martin OC and that well known consortium the Eight Clubs (attended by 2,000 spectators and their 400-plus cars); and many lessons had been learned by MCC observers attending these meetings, to be applied to their forthcoming meeting in September (see Chapter 9).

The important announcement was made in the Press early in June 1950 that the Club proposed to revert immediately to its pre-war scale of activities – the first major event to be the *Exeter* in January 1951. One can almost sense the feelings of enthusiasm and excitement in the Minutes of the Exeter Trial sub-committee meeting held on 14 August 1950 – with Jackie Masters in the chair. It was decided to run it on lines almost identical to the 1939 event with a night section of 150 miles from three starting points to Exeter,

1959: Bob Garland and his father make a spirited climb of Hustyn in the *Land's End*. Bob is in the sidecar whilst his father, who first competed in MCC events driving a Salmson in 1924, conducts the Ariel.

'LAND'S END' 1959

1970: With passenger Nigel Nichols putting his all into bouncing, Dennis Scobey's Dellow scrabbles away from the re-start test near the summit of Bluehills Mine in the Land's End Trial – making a clean climb, and securing his Gold Medal.

followed by the trial proper. Two of these starts, Virginia Water (London) and Stratford-on-Avon, were as in 1939, but Plymouth replaced Exeter as the third. Deller's Cafe, familiar to thousands of *Exeter* competitors, was again listed as the breakfast halt; and all the old familiar hills were included – Windout, Fingle, Simms, Higher Rill, Pin Hill, Harcombe and Meerhay, with the finish at the Grand Hotel, Bournemouth. Closing date for entries was set for 4 December.

Any suggestion that the Club was reactionary or adopting an unprogressive attitude was forestalled in pre-event publicity by emphasising that the trial was being run in its old form principally to introduce the MCC type of event to a new generation of competitors. In retrospect, this 'excuse' seemed scarcely necessary as today, thirty-nine years on, the *Exeter*, *Land's End* and to a degree the *Edinburgh* are still run to their old form – and still attract enormous entries. This view was further emphasised by the entry for that first full-scale post-war *Exeter* which closed at 256 – 69 solos, 14 sidecars, 4 three-wheelers and 169 cars.

When the time came for surveying the proposed *Exeter* route, surprisingly little deterioration seemed to have occurred on the old hills during their years of idleness. Fingle had developed a large transverse rut which was easily repaired; Windout and Pin Hill were in very bad repair and had to be omitted – but the others were ready and waiting. The old way of running the event, that had proved successful through the years, was resumed, with the Clerk of the Course and his assistant chosen from among MCC officials, three elected Stewards, and an army of volunteer labour, provided in part by local car and motor-cycle clubs to serve as timekeepers at the several controls and timed sections, and also as observers and 'pushers-and-pullers' at the observed sections. Several lessons were learned, though, to be applied to the *Land's End* at Easter and subsequent classic trials. Notable among these was the need for more Land-Rovers, tractors and suchlike to clear failures from observed sections and avoid lengthy delays; and some sort of 'walkie-talkie' communication between observers on the 'Start' line and those unsighted farther up the section – to avoid sending competitors up a hill already blocked by a failure.

With the motor-cycle membership in mind the idea of organising a motor-cycle rally – as distinct from a trial – was again considered, with the somewhat surprising innovation of allowing pillion passengers to be carried (presumably as navigators). Again, though, the Scarborough club saved the Committee the trouble of setting up this event – having, for the second time, published their regulations for such a rally and then cancelling it through lack of entries. The motor-cycle fraternity it seemed were not in favour of a long and undemanding ride, punctuated by braking and wiggle-woggle tests.

Always on the look-out for further ways of entertaining the membership, the Committee had spent much time at their wartime meetings in discussions about running sheer speed, as distinct from regularity, reliability or sporting, events. The possibility of acquiring a suitable site for a short racing circuit had been considered, as well as one for a speed hill-climb on the lines of Shelsley Walsh and Prescott. Though this was a change in policy, it was agreed to approach the Bugatti Owner's Club, whose Prescott Hill near Cheltenham had recently been made available for hire to clubs, though no applications were as yet made for specific dates.

In January 1951 the Committee moved to The Bull and Mouth, in London's Bloomsbury, for their twice-monthly meetings, and plans went ahead for the *Land's End* at Easter (23–24 March). Three starting points were chosen – Plymouth, Virginia Water and Stratford-on-Avon, as in the *Exeter*, with breakfast and lunch stops at Taunton and Bude. Grabhurst Hill was added to what had been basically the 1939 route; Doverhay, having deteriorated, was used for motor-cycle classes alone, and Station Hill, Lynmouth, was omitted. The ever-present matter of the 'doctoring' of Beggars' Roost by the local Council, making it more 'interesting' for the hundreds of spectators who lined the hill and perched like birds in the bare trees, was discussed. Since this involved importing lorry loads of loose stones and large rocks to a climb that was already difficult enough, it was decided to approach them respectfully and ask them to desist – a very difficult decision as the well-being of all three classic trials depended, and still depends, so much on the enthusiasm and co-operation of local authorities. The problem continues annually. Time allowances at checks were altered, permitting no early arrival and an increase in acceptable lateness. A new *Land's End* award was presented by long-time MCC member A. G. d'A. Sugden to encourage the use of 'vintage' motor-cycles in the event, minor concessions being made for these old war-horses, including the use of the old Bluehills course, instead of the much tougher new one.

Already the entry was creeping back to pre-war levels, with a total of 337 – 153 motor-cycle classes and 184 cars. In the event, car performances on Darracott were ignored as the tractor broke down and later car entries had to bypass the hill. Nancy Mitchell, who was already becoming very well known in international rallies, told Major Marians with charming diffidence at the finish that, as she could not lay claim to a Premier Award (a 'Gold'), and

1964: Proudly displaying his BRDC badge, though having by now given best to the advancing years and advanced to the luxury of four wheels, de Mattos makes light work of Tillerton in the Exeter Trial.

1952: North Devon farmer Ray Easterbrook picks a careful path up Darracott in the *Land's End* on his 500T Norton – a splendid trials motor-cycle in its day – his concentration helped no doubt by the then near-obligatory cigarette.

could not therefore win a 'Triple Award' for penalty-free performances in all three classic events, she would not enter the *Edinburgh*. As it turned out, she had in fact won a 'Gold'.

The trial had been a tough one, with 85 retirements, 57 'no awards' and only 61 claiming 'Golds'; there were 29 non-starters. Again there were lessons to be learned, including the need for a Travelling Marshal to precede the competitors in order to hand out programmes to the Police, and the AA and RAC officials on duty; and the inadvisability of starting motor-cycle entries at half-minute intervals with the possibility of having two on a section at the same time.

Apart from the classic trials, other events were added to the Club's programme including the popular Continental Tour (this time to Austria), an Isle of Wight Rally, the traditional Opening Run in February; and of course, the traditional Team and Sporting trials. Added to their own calendar, the Club was being invited by increasing numbers of other clubs to compete in their events; among those accepted were the Lancashire AC's Morecambe Rally, the MGCC's Cockshoot Trial for cars, and the Southern Sporting Trial for motor-cycles. It was decided, however, that the *Edinburgh* should not yet be reinstated in its full glory, but would run as a rally with solo motor-cyclists carrying pillion passengers if they wanted to.

Entries closed at 117, with 29 solos, 7 sidecars, 1 three-wheeler and 80 cars. Although Arthur Bourne was editor of *Motor Cycle*, and had served the MCC faithfully for some 25 years, his journal published – in the Committee's opinion – 'a very insignificant report which did not do the event justice'. His leading article (and a letter which the Committee felt had been 'inspired') were also critical. That such a respected journalist should have criticised the event, despite his involvement, must have indicated that something was amiss.

What with the Silverstone meeting in September (see Chapter 9), the Sporting Trial in October, the Inter-Club Trial, the time-consuming *Daily Express* Rally (see Chapter 8) in November and the *Exeter* at the close of the year, the Committee were able to do little more in celebration of the Club's 1951 Golden Jubilee than to organise a special Golden Jubilee Dinner on 23 November, to which H. S. Linfield, editor of *The Autocar*, was invited as principal guest. This dinner was also significant in marking the end of the first full year of sporting events. Suddenly the frustrations of the early post-war years seemed long ago.

1954: Since the thirties the Army has used MCC trials as a training ground – one of their official entries being Maurice Arden, seen tackling Hustyn's rocky slopes in the *Land's End*. Now a middle-aged businessman, Maurice rides a modern trail bike in MCC events.

1977: Current Chairman John Aley climbs strongly on the lower reaches of Simms, in his diminutive Fiat 126, one of the smaller cars competing in MCC events. Farther up this notorious 'stopper' a bank got in its way.

Rounding off the year, the *Exeter* was not without its difficulties as a great storm passed over Britain during the night of 28 December, transforming the night part of the trial from Plymouth, Stratford-on-Avon and Virginia Water to Exeter into a hazardous adventure. A deluge of rain, punctuated by driving snow and sleet flooded the roads during the wild night – though the day that followed, with the Exeter-to-Bournemouth section over Dartmoor and including many famous trials hills, was blue-skied and sunny. Fingle was the first section, washed clean of mud by the deluge but very slippery on the rock outcrops, which stopped many cars – including Cottle's Lancia Aprilia despite the passenger's efforts to grab overhanging bushes and haul the car uphill. Simms followed with the Morgan team shooting up 1–2–3 on perfect climbs, and the big Allards burbling up effortlessly. Higher Rill, Knowle Lane, Stonelands and Cocknowle featured in the list of observed sections.

The field of over 140 cars and 117 motor-cycles produced the usual wide variety of types and ages, including Bill Boddy's and N. A. Smith's aged, belt-driven Tamplin and several of the new post-war integral-construction $1^1/_2$-2 litre family saloons which proved to be well up to the traditional type of MCC trial. And, of course, the several one-off specials, with their light weight and purpose-designed weight distribution, did well – at the cost of a miserably exposed night's drive down to Exeter.

From the earliest days the Temple Press journals *Motor Cycling* and *The Motor* and their Iliffe counterparts the *Motor Cycle* and *The Autocar* (on which I was editorially involved during the fifties, sixties and seventies) had given excellent coverage to these events. We would set out at night, journalist and photographer, from one or other of the starting points and accompany the competitors right through to the finish, stopping to watch and photograph their performances on as many observed sections as possible. We took it all very seriously and the resulting accounts in the following week's issue would occupy anything up to four pages. We – and particularly I, having been

1955: One of the *Exeter*'s best-loved and longest-used hills, Fingle Bridge starts down by the river Teign at a well-known beauty spot. Here, Allin Penhale climbs strongly in his Ford Ten special, with brother-in-law George Edwards as bouncer.

1968: Like the Army, many years before, the Police have entered teams in MCC trials since the sixties – instituted by Inspector Alec Smith, seen having a 'dab' as he climbs Bluehills on a normal white-tank Police Triumph motorcycle.

weaned on these events – felt that, with so many spectators crowding the observed sections (an estimated 15,000 at Bluehills Mine) and fields of over 400 sometimes, there was ample public interest to demand full coverage. As sports editor from 1955 to 1968, I did my best to continue this policy, though it was against increasing pressure from above. So many successful specialist sporting journals had appeared since the war that there was little point, it was felt, in wide-based motoring journals such as ours trying to compete with the specialists. It was a policy I could never understand, even in later years as editor of *Autocar* (the definite article had been dropped in 1962). Though sporting events in the true sense, the MCC's classic trials were essentially for the ordinary motorist in his ordinary car – which was precisely the readership catered for by *Autocar*. Eventually in the late sixties coverage of the classics was abandoned altogether; we left it to the specialists, which I think was a mistake – if for no other reason than that it is now necessary to buy two motoring journals each week.

The traditional Sporting Trial, scheduled for October 1951, was thought to be losing its appeal to MCC members, and various alterations were suggested by the British Trials and Rally Drivers' Association to bring it into line with other trials in their Gold Star competition. It was agreed that the suggestions should be considered but that it would be better not to include it in their list of qualifying events at least for 1951.

Settling back to their pre-war pattern of events, the Club set the 1952 activities in motion on 2 March with the Opening Run, held on Hunsdon Aerodrome near Bishops Stortford, with driving/riding tests and various indoor entertainments. What the 1952 *Land's End* sub-committee can have been thinking about when they proposed allowing pillion passengers to be carried on solo motor-cycles is not known, but the decision was wisely reversed by the main Committee. S. C. H. ('Sammy') Davis, for nearly 40 years Sports Editor of *The Autocar* and a regular competitor in MCC trials, was invited to serve as Steward, along with F. A. Appleby, one-time editor of the journal. And, using the old 1927 route – which was perhaps familiar to some of them in their heyday – the Vintage Sports Car Club and Vintage MCC entered 4 contingents of old cars and motor-cycles bringing the total entry of cars and motor-cycles to more than 400.

The Vintage cars ran at the front of the field, separated from their modern counterparts by the whole field of motor-cycles. They were spared Grabhurst, first of the trials hills, but were faced by timed climbs of Porlock and Lynmouth hills, both of which, with their steep gradients and very poor surfaces, had been 'stoppers' when the cars were young. The infamous Beggars' Roost was the first of their potential problems, taken in darkness and included in their itinerary because it had been in use in the *Land's End* since the early twenties, and should have been familiar to them. Nigel Arnold-Forster's 1926 Trojan picked its way up delicately at constant, though slow speed; Routledge's 1924 Morris made the climb more quickly, but Grace's 1923 twin-cylinder Jowett failed to live up to the old company's slogan of being able to climb anything.

The motor-cycle contingent mostly climbed easily – and Denis Scobey's J2 Allard, heralding the modern cars, shot up as though it was a speed hill-climb to the delight of the huge crowds that had gathered. Barton Steep followed, with its special tests; and Doverhay was omitted for the car entry, its rock outcrops reckoned to be too damaging to everyday family cars. Darracott's many turns and damp, earthy surface presented no problems. As in the previous *Exeter*, the post-war crop of small, family saloons such as the Austin A40 made an excellent showing. There was a very interesting lesson to be learned from the way in which the cars and motor-cycles ranging in date from the early twenties to ultra-modern with thirty years' additional development, were putting up pretty similar performances on the same hills, each age-group finding them as easy (or difficult) as the other. What is more, most of the hills confronting them had been in use as observed sections continuously since the old cars first took to the roads . . .Crackington, New Mill, Hustyn, Bluehills and the rest.

The year 1952 brought increasing numbers of invitations from other clubs to compete in their events, including the West Hants and Dorset CC's race meeting at Ibsley – and one from the Bugatti OC for four MCC members to offer themselves as a team at one of their Prescott hill-climb meetings. By June there were so many of these invitations that the Committee started turning them down. In a more domestic field, a quotation was received from the Caxton Name Plate Co for a gross of cast bronze MCC badges – at 8s 6d (45p) apiece; a gross was ordered, to be passed on to members at 15s (75p). Dingley and Co were also approached over the possibility of getting the present badge down to 2oz in die-stamped brass (the maximum permitted weight for articles produced by this method). They produced an identical badge though

1983: Chief Official Allin Penhale looks on as Boyce's Frazer Nash navigates the water-splash at the foot of Crackington during the *Land's End*. The depth of this 'splash' is unpredictable – dependent upon the damming operations of the locals.

1954: A perfect 'special'? The Tucker-MG is shown climbing Fingle on its way to a 'Gold' in the *Exeter*; a few months later it won a race at the Silverstone meeting. At first a two-seater, it was later extended to accommodate the two Tucker-Peake daughters as they grew up – until another special was built for their use.

lighter in weight; 200 were ordered. Today's badges cost £10.

The *Edinburgh*, still run as a rally at Whitsun, continued to attract only relatively small fields; for 1952 it totalled 152 (52 motor-cycles; 100 cars). Three control points were used for the Whit Saturday start – London, Bristol and Burton – the overnight routes of roughly similar length converging on Harrogate for the breakfast halt. A succession of driving, regularity and braking tests punctuated the common route via the Pennines, Lake District and other wild country to Keswick, Newlands Hause, Carlisle and the main-road run to the finish at Edinburgh – whence several competitors immediately set off to compete at the Goodwood Whit Monday meeting. As with the *Land's End*, there were several entries from the Army Motor Cycling Association; a few had also taken part in the Sunbeam 200 Trial and had been reported by the scrutineers as being 'in a shocking condition'!

Though the MCC's policy has always been to cater for the tastes of every type of member – and there is always fun to be had in any competitive event on two, three or four wheels – somehow as a competitor one found this rally-type *Edinburgh* oddly atypical of the MCC, and a poor relation of its predecessors. There were already many small clubs running similar events at the time and people didn't join the mature and respected MCC to compete in them – splendid though they were as training-grounds before embarking on major National and International rallies.

By June 1952 the paid-up membership had increased to 554 car owners and 292 motor-cyclists – a total of 846 with a further 322 (220 cars and 112 motor-cycles) who had been asked firmly though politely to pay up – or else. . . . The single Club typewriter with which the Secretary had been authorised to provide himself back in 1909 was now proving inadequate for Mrs Harris who, for years, had done the Club's secretarial work. Unless the *Daily Express* could provide one on loan (on the strength of the MCC's involvement with the ongoing *Daily Express* Rally), it was agreed to hire one until the work eased. The Finance Committee were nothing if not parsimonious! New offices at 76 Kinnerton Street, London SW1 – an address that was to become familiar to members over many years – were taken over on 31 July 1950, the cost of the

The Misses Tucker-Peake – Maralyn and Susan – about to leave the start-line on Bluehills Mine in the 'Tucker Nipper Special'.

move from Bloomsbury coming to £26.

Motor sport in all its forms was taking off. In July 1952 the Secretary (Jackie Masters) was approached by the Hastings Town Clerk and Councillor Mr Sims-Hilditch with a view to constructing a race-circuit at Hastings on ground owned by the Corporation. Masters said he was certain the MCC would like to become involved and a deputation from the Committee was selected to meet Hastings Corporation officials for further talks. Though several dates through August and September seem to have been offered – and declined – there is no record of this meeting having ever taken place, or of what became of such an ambitious idea – except that it was stillborn.

In August came the disastrous flood in the Lynmouth area, with houses, cars, bridges and whatever stood in its path swept away, some of them into the sea. Much of the area within the triangle South Molton–Barnstaple–Lynmouth was devastated – and cut off for some days. Not only was it an extremely popular holiday centre, but it was 'MCC country' too. Members felt themselves almost personally involved and a Lynmouth Relief Fund was set up by the Club – to which they contributed almost £600.

The route for the 1953 *Exeter*, held on 2–3 January, included the following observed hills: Gittisham, Fingle, Waterworks, Simms, Strete's, Knowle Lane and Afflington – seven in contrast with the fourteen climbed by competitors in the 1988 event, and of those only Fingle and Simms are still in use. The event produced an entry of 325 (125 solos, 31 sidecars, 3 three-wheelers and 166 cars), an increase of 66 over 1952. Despite reports of previous post-war MCC classic trials in such as *The Autocar*, stating unequivocally that the post-war family saloons were well-suited to the events in their current form, Committee member R. C. Porter expressed the view that they were not; and the Secretary, none other than the experienced Jackie Masters, agreed, and said that he had been criticised for adhering to the 'official line' that the events were 'suitable for standard cars'. In retrospect, the views of these two authorities must have created quite a stir among Committee members, though they seem odd – at least insofar as the mass-produced, bread-and-butter cars were concerned, with their good ground clearances and low first gears. Certainly some of the more exotic high-performance sports cars and grand tourers, with their minimal clearance and high axle-ratios were very unsuitable – and it was up to their owners not to enter them. In any case, not a lot of attention seems to have been paid to these views, for the old familiar list of test-hills appeared on the *Land's End* route card for Easter – Stoney Street, Doverhay, Station Lane, Beggars' Roost, Darracott, Crackington, New Mill, Hustyn and Bluehills Mine. Grabhurst and Barton Steep were omitted.

A welcome letter from the Clerk of the Lynton and Lynmouth UDC

1978: Competing here in the *Land's End*, Lewis Oliver's Oliver Special was based largely on Dellow where Oliver was employed, during the late 1940s. After being virtually scrapped it was rebuilt by John West, who is driving it here.

thanked the Club gratefully for their contribution to the Relief Fund – and, to the relief of the *Land's End* sub-committee, reassured them that there would be no problems if the route were to follow its usual course through the area. With the so-called '*Exeter*' finishing at Bournemouth, and the *Edinburgh* now a rally (though finishing at Edinburgh) there was talk in the Committee of finishing the *Land's End* at Truro. This was not especially in order to omit the main-road extra mileage from Bluehills Mine to the finish but because of the almost complete ignoring of the event, and the increased trade it had for so many years brought annually to the area, by the Penzance civic authorities. The MCC classic events, with their vast entries and armies of officials that brought perhaps 500-odd people for a night's rest into the areas in which they finished, were accustomed to some sort of civic reception – not a myopic-to-blind eye. It was decided, for the time being at least, to continue with the finish at Land's End.

Despite the Committee decision that the VSCC and VMCC should not be invited to compete, as they had been in 1952, the *Land's End* entry reached a post-war record of 426 (226 solos, 31 sidecars, 3 three-wheelers and 166 cars).

The work involved in checking the performances by 426 competing vehicles on eight observed sections, together with any penalty points incurred for late arrival at controls, was truly formidable and it was decided that in future six people should be appointed, at least two of whom must be available to work every evening following the event until the results had been calculated. As things stood it was difficult enough; with the addition of the elderly cars and motor-cylces it would have been almost impossible.

As for the trial itself, that 'farmers delight', a promising red sky on Good Friday night, was thoroughly misleading as the 125-mile night run from Virginia Water, Launceston and Kenilworth to the breakfast stop at Taunton brought heavy falls of snow, fog, and stinging sleet and rain showers – which, along with a south-westerly gale in their faces, also accompanied competitors throughout the day. Beggars' Roost had been over-dressed in rocks and stones by the local enthusiasts – right from the start line this time; they usually show some consideration by leaving a few yards clear, to build up speed. More than

The versatility of the Morgan is well suited to MCC events. KUY474 was an early 'Flat front' Vanguard-engined Plus Four and appeared in the 1952 National rally driven by Jacky Ray and a few years later in Tom Threlfall's hands in the *Exeter*, as shown here.

25 per cent of the entry fell victim to their hazards.

Looking back through the reports of this 1953 *Land's End* one can see how wrong Bob Porter was in referring to the unsuitability of modern family cars. There are repeated references to 'fine climbs' of the various observed sections by such cars – and of failures by the XK120 Jaguars which, as *The Autocar* pointed out, was ' . . .a model never designed to be a trials car'. In summing-up the event, *The Autocar* (which was me, as I covered the trial) said: 'Three categories alone are not really suitable – the very long, large car; modern cars that are very nose-heavy; and small cars that do not have either a low bottom gear or a modification for extra power.' In retrospect, this comment still seems about right, though perhaps we should have said: 'Modern cars that are nose-heavy – and whose entrants have not troubled to put some ballast, such as their passengers and an extra spare wheel, at the back.'

An interesting point arose after this event concerning the sidecar entries. Out of an entry of 34, only one First Class Award and one Second had been awarded and it was felt they had been unduly penalised. It was eventually agreed, after much research, that the standard of riding must have deteriorated since much better performances had been put up by sidecar entries on the selfsame hills 20 and more years ago.

The *Edinburgh*, run as usual at Whitsun, was steadily gaining strength as a rally, now with increased entries. The 457-mile route from the Rouncil Towers Motel at Kenilworth and finishing at Edinburgh was shrouded almost throughout its length by rain – which must have played a major part in the retirement of nearly 50 per cent of the motor-cycle entries. The results were decided by the many tests: Fast-Slow at Oughtershaw; Brake Test on the north side of Buttertubs Pass; Stop-and-Re-start at Stonesdale; Regularity Test on Tan Hill; Regularity Test on Hardknott and Wrynose passes; Stop-and-Re-start on the Tweedsmuir-Tibble Shiels section; and a Triple Stop-Re-start test at the finish at Edinburgh. This consisted of three stops and re-starts in quick succession against the clock. The lines astride which we had to stop were just too far apart for comfort in first gear and were too close for a change-up into second – resulting in frightful over-revving and load-reversals in the transmission! And there was a time limit of 30 seconds. W. A. G. Goodall's Morgan Plus Four and G. A. Lewis's Silverstone Healey were very fast, taking only 24 $^4/_5$ seconds.

During 1953 L. A. Baddeley, President and one of the names that will for ever be associated with the MCC (see Chapter 12) was forced to retire through ill health. In proposing the election of Sir Algernon Guinness, Bart. as the new President, the Chairman paid tribute to Baddeley ' . . .for the wonderful work he had done for the Club, both as Treasurer and President, over a period of forty-eight years'. Baddeley's retirement came as a very personal loss to the older members.

Undeterred by the increasing annual programme of events – and the increasing number of events in which members were being invited to compete by other clubs (including the Bugatti Owners, who again invited the MCC to send a team to Prescott) – the Committee applied to the ACU for a date in September for a motor-cycle race meeting at the Crystal Palace. In anticipation of very large numbers of London spectators, it was felt that a really important programme should be laid on – though one or two committee members wondered whether the Club would have sufficient time, in view of their many other commitments. It was a case of the busiest people being the ones with time to take on more, and plans went ahead – only to be abandoned when the permit was not granted – for reasons which are not recorded. With the additional work involved in running the important *Daily Express* Rally, the Committee were very busy indeed at the time; the decision must have come as a relief to many.

It is recorded in the 26 November 1953 Minutes that: 'In view of the congestion at the Club's office caused by the Autumn Trial and *Daily Express* Rally entry lists closing the same week, it was suggested that the Autumn Trial entries might be handled by a sub-committee at a different address.'

CHAPTER 7

Fair for Everyone?

There can not have been many clubs – if indeed any – who, at the close
of 1953, were making plans for the following year to celebrate the 50th
Anniversary of one of their sporting events; but it was so with the MCC
and their 'Edinburgh Run', first held in May 1904. A 'feeler' was sent, to all
members and to the Press in February, seeking reactions to holding the event
on 21–22 May as a special anniversary run with the route and conditions as
nearly as possible identical to those of the 1904 'Run', and the entry open to
all members, past and present, riding or driving any type of vehicle of any age.

The response was good and at one minute past eight on the evening of 21
May the first of 48 entries (34 cars and 14 motor-cycles) set off northwards
from the GPO London – just as their forebears had done so many years
ago. Twenty-four hours later all but three had completed the 397 miles to
Edinburgh. The two oldest cars, Roy Clarkson's 1902 Panhard-et-Levassor and
J. E. Ford's 1907 Lanchester, retired respectively at Hitchin and Grantham.
But despite heavy rain and a bitter wind the old vehicles did well including
R. Gore's diminutive 6hp Le Zebre and George Simpson's 1910 Model T Ford.

Among the older competitors (as distinct from the vehicles) was A. E.
Bowyer-Lowe who, at over seventy, had been driving since 1899 and had
taken part in his first *Edinburgh* in 1905. This time he enjoyed a dry,
warm and wholly uneventful run in his Ford Consul – haunted by ghostly
visions through the wiper-blades' arcs of the old, rutted Great North Road,
horse-drawn vehicles, roadside inns and sleeping villages – unaware as yet of

THE MOTOR CYCLING CLUB, Ltd. RETURN. **3**

LONDON—EXETER and Back Run—December 26th and 27th, 1924.

Standard Time	Competitor's Own Time	Place	Mileage	Total Mileage	Checking Points	Route and Instructions
a.m. 7.30	10.26	EXETER ...	0	162	SIGN at Garage.	Return to Garage from Deller's, in time for punctual start. Proceed up Paris Street and follow tramlines. About ½ mile beyond tram terminus L at road fork, and by main road through Rockbeare to Honiton.
8.18	11.14	Honiton ...	16	178	NON-STOP BEGINS.	Beyond Moor's Carage turn R opposite church, up New Street for ascent of Marlpits Hill, leaving station and church on R.
8.22	11.18	MARLPITS HILL, TOP	1¼	179¼	CHECK. NON-STOP ENDS. Sign beyond Summit.	Non-stop ends, and check at Old Marlpit Gate. Turn R at this d.p., and along ridge of Farway Hill.
8.36	11.32	Roncombe Gate	4½	183¾		Just beyond fork road at Roncombe Gate R at unmarked byway, and descend Hatway Hill. At foot L, and straight on twice, avoiding the turns to Sidbury Village on right.
8.45	11.41	Sidbury (near)	2¾	186½		R at next fork, cross main road at foot of Trow Hill and by Sid, to beginning of Sidmouth, where turn L to foot of Salcombe Hill.
8.53	11.49	Salcombe Hill, Foot	2¾	189¼	NON-STOP BEGINS.	
8.56	11.52	SALCOMBE HILL, TOP	¾	190	CHECK. NON-STOP ENDS. Sign at Summit.	Straight on from summit. L at Memorial Cross. Join main road from Exeter. At 19th m.s. keep L, ½ m. later R. Avoid the Seaton Road and descend to village.
9.22	12.18	Colyford ...	8½	198½		Beyond sta., and river bridge, in ¼ mile, L at Boshill (leaving Lyme Road), and follow "A 374" through Musbury.
9.37	12.3[illegible]	Axminster ...	5	203½	CHECK.	Entering Axminster, check and turn R at Mr. Vince's Axminster Garage along Lyme Street. Petrol available. In ¼ mile sharp L at fork marked Seektor, just before Lamb Inn; and after Stammery Hill join 3165 to Marshwood and Birdsmoor Gate.
9.57	[illegible].53	Birdsmoor Gate	6¾	210¼		At Birdsmoor Gate take obscure square R turn, leave 3165 and follow 3164.
10. 8	1.4	Broadwindsor	3½	213¾		R. In village, again R at White Lion. At cross roads, straight on, leave 3164 and take 3163.
10.17	[illegible]	Beaminster ...	3	216¾		At Red Lion, in centre of town, turn L for White Sheet Hill.
		WHITE SHEET HILL	—	—	STOP and RESTART. NON-STOP BEGINS.	Midway up the hill, COMPULSORY STOP at line. RESTART by flag signal. Second line, 20 yds. on, to be reached in 15 secs. Non-stop from that line to summit.
10.23	1.19	Summit of Hill	1¼	218	NON-STOP ENDS.	Beyond summit R at direction post to Maiden Newton and Dorchester.
10.47	1.43	Maiden Newton	8	226		Follow main road through.
11. 8	2.4	DORCHESTER	8	234	CHECK. No Signatures.	Entering bear R. **Petrol, Oil, &c., at Churchill's Garage, The Grove.** Five minutes allowed for coffee, as Mr. W. G. Churchill's guests.
11.13	2.9	do. (depart)	—	—		
p.m. 12. 4	3.0	Blandford ...	16	250		1½ miles past Dorchester keep L. In Puddletown turn sharp L, then straight on. On reaching Blandford turn R after crossing river, then bear L and ascend Salisbury Street.
12.40	3.36	Woodyates Inn	12	262		Unmistakable main road straight on.
1. 1	3.57	Coombe Bisset	7	269		Straight on.
1.10	4.6	SALISBURY ...	3	272	CONTROL and CHECK. Sign at White Hart.	On entering City follow main road to **White Hart Hotel,** for Lunch. Enter Hotel from St. Ann's Street entrance of yard

The comparison of the route cards for the 1924 London-Exeter and for the same event in 1985, sixty-one years later, shows little change. The route may have altered slightly to cater for the changing vehicles, but the layout and the form of instructions differ little.

the awakening they were to receive in the coming days of motoring for the masses, yet already gratefully employing as chicken-houses the elegant bodies of disused coaches and carriages rendered obsolete by the snowballing onrush of mechanised transport. In the gentle, unhurried manner of its running, the 1954 *Edinburgh* was a link with the past that brought back many memories.

. . .

The *Exeter* at the start of the new year had already come and gone. It had been a memorable event for me as Peter Morgan had generously (and trustingly) lent me his convertible-bodied Morgan Plus Four, JNP 239, 'Gold' winning veteran of many MCC events in Peter's hands. Compared with the all-time record of 427 in 1925, there were 302 entries – 136 solos, 26 sidecars, 5 three-wheelers and 135 cars. There should also have been several more entries from the Army Motoring Cycling Association (as there were in most of the MCC trials at the time) but some had been refused owing to late

Standard Time	Competitor's Time	Place	Mileage	Total Mileage	Route and Instructions
		BICKINGTON			Q Continue through village, down hill passing garage, and just before bottom of hill, R by white house, under bridge and immediately R up hill, and in 2 miles S.O. at staggered X road, d.p. Ilsington and Haytor. In ½ mile fork R, S.O. at bottom of hill around sharp R hand corner. CARE, and S.O. to
		ILSINGTON	3½	85½	On entering village, sharp R and past cottages down lane "Unsuitable Q for Motors" to
08.30		**SIMMS**	½	86	OBSERVED SECTION No. 7, and CAT B RESTART. At summit, S.O. to
08.35		**SIMMS CONTROL 'OUT'**	¼	86¼	L at staggered X road, down narrow track and steep rough hill, CARE, to
		OLD TOWN WOOD	¼	86½	SPECIAL TEST No. 2. After test, continue along track to major road where CARE, R and continue along major road to
		LIVERTON	1½	88	S.O. through village, SLOW AND QUIET, S.O. at X road by Garage. Q In 1 mile L onto old A38, d.p. Newton Abbot, A382 to
		DRUMBRIDGES ROUNDABOUT	1½	89½	Continue around roundabout and take 2nd. exit L, d.p. Exeter, A38 onto dual carriageway (Caution. Later competitors will be traversing the R'bout en route to Simms). Continue along dual carriageway for about ¾ mile, taking 3rd. exit L onto slip road, d.p. Chudleigh Knighton and Kingsteignton. R at top of slip road. Continue round bends over narrow hump bridge, and R at T. Past claypits and S.O. at roundabout, and continue to
		KINGSTEIGNTON	4½	94	At T junction in town, turn R, d.p. Newton Abbot, and in ¼ mile L by Q Kings Arms. In 200 yards keep L at roundabout, under bypass, and take exit, d.p. Torbay, A380. Join dual carriageway, crossing river Teign, and in 1½ miles L at roundabout and take 1st. exit, d.p. Shaldon and Combe-In-Teignhead. Shortly R along St. Marychurch Road, passing Garage, up hill through wooded avenue, and in 2 miles take 3rd. L, d.p. Rocombe, down steep narrow hill. S.O. at staggered junction to T, where L by farm and R to
09.15		**SLIPPERY SAM**	6	100	OBSERVED SECTION No.8, and CAT. B RESTART. Continue after section ends to X road, (muddy lane), where R. (GREAT CARE -NARROW ROADS) In ½ mile. L at major road, A379. In 2½ miles down winding hill, and at bottom, L, d.p. Teignmouth and Dawlish.
		TEIGNMOUTH	3	103	Enter town via long bridge over estuary, R at traffic lights, d.p. Town Q Centre, Dawlish and Exeter. In ½ mile L at next traffic lights, d.p. Exeter B3192 (A38). In 4 miles L, d.p. A380, over bridge and R, A380 to join dual carriageway (CARE). Continue S.O. to join M5.
		M5 MOTORWAY Junction 30	9 4	112 116	Continue on Motorway to junction No. 30, where leave the motorway, d.p. Exeter, A379. At roundabout, keep R around and leave by A3052, 4th. Exit d.p. Sidmouth. S.O. at next roundabout and continue on A3052 to
		NEWTON POPPLE FORD	8	124	Q

arrival. During a route survey early in December 1953, both Stonelands and Afflington were found to be in excessively bad condition – in fact, the Chairman's Standard Vanguard had suffered costly damage to its underside when making a leisurely descent of Afflington.

Of the three starting points that converged upon the common route from Honiton – Virginia Water, Kenilworth and Launceston – we chose the former. As ever with this mid-winter event, there was the air of anticipation and preparation – darkness, meeting old friends, wandering round inspecting the rival concerns, heavily wrapped-up crews of the open cars and motor-cycles, and misgivings about the possible hazards of ice, fog and the rest – all of which provoked wonderful feelings of adventure. We were fortunate in our choice as the Kenilworth starters had dense fog and icy roads down to the Bristol control and very few checked in on time.

Pin Hill, as a curtain-raiser, was easy, as was Windout, ten miles on from Exeter – except for a solo motor-cyclist whose machine capsized, caught fire and blazed merrily causing delays before the fire extinguishers could be found. The rider was unhurt. Fingle came next, first used by the MCC in 1932 and famous as a 'stopper' with its great length, rocky outcrops and nine hairpin corners, two of which are very steep. A deep gulley had been excavated on the first right-hander by digging-in left-side rear wheels and the surface was badly broken up. Our rising spirits were damped as we watched failure after failure – but when our turn came we managed not to let down the Morgan works team, all three of which rocketed up, as did the Earl of Northesk's Jaguar XK120.

Simms, though, with its average gradient of 1 in $3^1/_2$ – part of which steepens to 1 in $2^1/_2$ – was at its worst and by far the worst hill in the trial. Many failed even to reach the 'Section Begins' sign, and clean climbs were achieved pretty well exclusively by the Dellows and trials specials. Our own failure was inevitable; but it came as some comfort when we were told that W. A. G. Goodall's works Morgan Plus Four had also failed. The lengthy delays on Fingle and Simms put most of us a couple of hours late, but the remaining five hills were fairly easy – Stretes, Harcombe, Meerhay, Knowle Lane and Cucknowle – though the stop-and-re-start test on Cucknowle put paid to anticipated Premier Awards for a few who had 'cleaned' Fingle and Simms.

It was with some relief, as we checked in at the Grand Hotel Bournemouth, that we hadn't entirely brought shame upon the good name of Morgan – and that I hadn't bent Peter's car!

So far as the additional Army entries were concerned, excluded because their entries had been sent in too late, the MCC Secretary attended a committee meeting at the War Office. He drew attention to the number of Army entries that were regularly being received beyond the deadline, not only in the *Exeter*. A member of the Army committee explained that, so far as the *Exeter* had been concerned, it had been due entirely to an oversight in his department; he accepted 'entire responsibility for the unfortunate occurrence'. Taking advantage of this tactical gain, the MCC Secretary went on to suggesst that it would increase the Army riders' chances of winning awards if the Army MCA were to waive their in-house rule forbidding their riders to reduce tyre pressure on observed sections – like everybody else did. It was explained, however, that the Army were using these events – as they had been since before World War II – to help train despatch riders *in war conditions* when the enemy could not be relied upon to allow time for such activities. Whether they yielded or not is not known.

Tyres were very much in the minds of the Committee at the time. For the *Exeter*, motor-cycle competitors were allowed to use 'competition' tyres, which meant such as Dunlop Universals – but emphatically not snow tyres or the 'knobblies' that had been banned by the RAC back in 1939 because they carried too much mud on to the roads following an observed section. In February 1954 the RAC recommended that the MCC should adopt their 1949 regulations as far as cars were concerned. The ACU placed a maximum width limit of 4 inches for motor-cycles, with three-wheelers limited to the size fitted when the vehicle was new. A later letter from the ACU, whose first letter had been ambiguous, stated that they had intended to say 'The smallest size over 4 inches fitted as standard' – which also takes a bit of interpreting!

A Mr Underwood had been disqualified from the 1953 Autumn Trial for using non-permitted tyres, and had accepted the Stewards' ruling – though he subsequently wrote to say that a Mr Sharp, using precisely the same type of tyre in the *Exeter*, had won an award. A letter was written to Mr Sharp who confirmed that he had been on Michelin S and that the scrutineer had approved them, saying that his decision was in accordance with the RAC regulations. This altercation was finally resolved with Mr Underwood's protest being upheld. He was given the Autumn Trial award to which he was entitled.

1985: International trials rider of repute (he was an Ariel works team member for many years) Bob Ray returned to trials in later years in an MG Midget – seen here between the walls of Wolfscote, climbing strongly during the *Edinburgh*.

1987: This MZ rider concentrates hard, feet firmly on the footrests as he picks his way carefully to the top. Note the way in which supplies for himself and his machine are carried – illustrating the need for self-sufficiency in these events.

The extent to which the Club was – and always has been – having to care for their traditional hills is shown in G. Patrick's report on his route inspection prior to the 1954 *Land's End*: 'Darracott Hill has obviously had a good deal of water down it, with the result that, in places, our concrete patches are standing proud; but the surface is quite fair. My Ford Anglia failed low down with wheelspin but by reducing the rear tyre pressures to 16lb I got up without much difficulty non-stop.' And Basil de Mattos's report on the western sections said that the hump on Bluehills would have to be dug away. The preparation of these events is not limited to straightforward paperwork – it includes road-building too.

He also reported that it had been impossible for him to drive up Crackington, New Mill, Hustyn and Bluehills as they were covered in snow; and of Bluehills he wrote: 'Snow-covered and a lovely and unusual sight for this part' (in early February). Doverhay was reported as no longer practicable, and Crowcombe was introduced as the first hill after the converging point of the three separate routes at Taunton. Lengthy reports about the availability of tractors to haul failures to the summit of the various hills were included – the horses which in the past had stood patiently by, hour after hour, waiting to perform this task had now become redundant. Feeding arrangements for competitors were reported with some pretty scathing comments about the performance of cafes chosen in previous years – such as running out of food before even the entire motor-cycle entry had passed through. Route-marking arrangements, too, were criticised – though these have always seemed almost superfluous as the route cards provide extremely detailed instructions. And, in addition to 'doctoring' the hills, tampering with route-markers has always been part of the fun for those who enjoy watching competitors casting round in farmyards and up cul-de-sacs, trying to get back on to the route!

On the general subject of the hills used in MCC events and, in particular the practice of doctoring them, two very significant propositions were put up by that well known driver of Trojans, Squadron Leader A. F. Scroggs, at the 1954 AGM in March:

That the continued use of certain observed sections in the Club's trials is inconsistent with the declared policy of the Club to cater for all classes of vehicles; and that either (a) these sections should be eliminated as compulsory tests, or (b) the claim of suitability of vehicles of non-sporting type should be abandoned.

One of the declared aims of this Club is to encourage and cater for all classes of drivers and vehicles, and in recent years quite a large number of quite ordinary cars have entered. This in itself, is all to the good. Results show, however, that in certain cases, notably Simms Hill, only a very small proportion of such vehicles have been successful. In the last *Exeter* in particular, not a single car of what might be called ordinary type got up. This was not due to any exceptional circumstances such as abnormal weather (which can not be catered for) as the weather was good and the hill in normal condition for the time of year.

I am sure that a large number of members would, like me, be very sorry to see the last of Simms and other old friends, but it does seem to me unfair to encourage new members with the promise of a trial suitable for everyday vehicles, and the implication that any such vehicle well driven should be able to win a First Class Award – and then to include an obstacle practically impossible for them.

What is the answer? One is, of course, to divide competitors into 'sporting' and 'non-sporting', or some such classes, but this immediately raises the almost insuperable difficulty of definition. A better way, I suggest, would be to return to the principle of the 1938 *Exeter*, when Simms was optional for First Class Awards, and a special award given to those who climbed it. . . .

I have referred to Simms Hill as an outstanding example of what I mean, but there are other hills such as Beggars' Roost in a 'doped' condition to which the same might apply.

The second of Scroggs's propositions was equally provocative:

That the practice, sometimes adopted in the past, of making certain hills in trials artificially easier or more difficult, be abandoned, and all hills used in the state provided by Nature.

1985: A smiling Mike Furse picks his way carefully through the ford at the foot of Wolfscote, in the Edinburgh Trial – enjoying the sunshine after the rigours of an October night in a car with few concessions to luxury.

There are at least two cases where the practice mentioned has been adopted – Simms and Beggars' Roost. The former was made artificially easier in 1938 with the result that it became too easy even for those competing at that time; and Beggars' Roost has at times been doped with loads of earth and stones to make it more formidable. In principle I consider this undesirable for two reasons. Firstly, the effect of the alterations is not easy to forecast, with the result that neither the Committee nor (even more) the competitors know what to expect; and, secondly – and perhaps even more important – other organisations wishing to use the hill in its normal state can not do so until the effect of the MCC treatment has worn off. In the case of Simms, which used to be quite a serious obstacle, it was years before its former difficulty was restored; and even now some signs of metalling can still be seen.

If a difficult hill is required, then let us choose one that is naturally difficult; and if an easy one is wanted, there are plenty available without spoiling a good one.

The particular case of Bluehills Mine might cause trouble if the above suggestion were adopted, owing to the artificial hairpins at the bottom and the prepared re-starting patch at the top; but as the whole thing in this case is somewhat artificial and is well known, it might be considered as an exceptional case, or treated as a 'starred hill' as in my other proposition.

Once again the claim of 'suitable for everyday vehicles' was being questioned, and Scroggs' well reasoned and authoritative comments were directed at the very heart of the traditional MCC trials. His recommendations were discussed at length and were finally left in the hands of the Executive for consideration in the light of various and diverse opinions expressed by those present.

It is true that the Club itself has had little or no control through the years over the doctoring of, for example, Beggars' Roost. It occurs to this day; and with bulldozers now at their disposal the local enthusiasts have been able to make the old hill even more formidable – as was the case with the 1989 *Land's End*, when Beggars' Roost had to be omitted altogether from the Trial because of the excessive attentions of local enthusiasts. It must have been a great disappointment to them. This, as I have said before, is an ongoing and difficult problem because the success of the trials depends so much on the goodwill of the local people and police. Throughout the years this has been excellent; but if the Club were to adopt a heavy hand, forbidding this practice (and mounting a guard to ensure it could not happen), much of the goodwill could be lost.

It is true, too, that there have been isolated *Exeters*, *Land's Ends* and *Edinburghs* in which nobody has won a First Class Award – but invariably

1986: A modern three-wheeler – Tony Divey's Triking awaits its turn to attempt Bamford Clough in the *Edinburgh*. Being classified as sidecar outfits, three-wheeler passengers are allowed to dispose their weight advantageously, as shown!

competitors have agreed afterwards that they were challenging and enjoyable events. What matters is that they are not competing against each other but against the Club. There was no question, therefore, of an ES2 Norton competing against a 500T; or of a Dellow (or other trials special) competing against an Austin A40 – to quote a contemporary. Yet, on a route common to all, what is possible for one could be impossible for the other, and the tests have had to provide obstacles with a similar challenge to both – assuming equal rider/driver skills.

Short of resorting to the impossible extreme of including different sets of observed sections along the route to cater for each category of vehicle, it has been possible to adapt requirements on the common obstacles so that the same – or nearly the same – result is achieved.

Justification of the claim that the MCC trials are suitable for everyday cars and motor-cycles has always been in the Committee's minds; and, as the categories and classes are divided at present, this is approximately so – provided that the vehicle is sensibly prepared and conducted. It is fair to say, however, that some vehicles are better suited to the conditions, and the man who has a car or motor-cycle which is kept and prepared specially for the events will stand a better chance. Against this, though, during reconnaissances of the route, officials regularly climb the observed sections in their everyday cars with no special preparation – no raising of the suspension, no sump shield or other underbody protection, and no special tyres.

MCC members can be divided into the following categories:
1. The Expert, who drives or rides regularly in trials and probably follows the championship trail, taking part in a dozen or more events during the year. About twenty per cent.
2. The Occasional Entrant in MCC and local events. Say thirty per cent.
3. The MCC Man who has probably been competing in these events on and off for most of his life, and probably does not enter any other events. Say twenty-five per cent.
4. The Beginner, who is probably in only his first or second event and will graduate into one of the categories. Twenty five per cent.

Originally there were no classes, but to equal things out they have gradually been introduced. Initially, cars were divided into Open and Closed categories;

1987: Chris Reeson's Troll is a typical modern front-engined special, popular for many years in MCC events. Small, adequately powerful, with good ground clearance and plenty of traction, this type is always in the running for a prize.

1987: John Teague's 2CV Citroen has plenty of 'applied' weight at the front to offset the weight transfer to the rear wheels on stiff climbs – an inherent handicap of front-drive cars, which are placed by the MCC regulations in a special category.

then Specials were put separately until today's regulations were introduced. These classes have done their job well, but the Club introduced a new set of classes in 1988 (See Appendix 4). These follow quite closely what were already in force but remove some of the anomalies. For example, 'Specials' had hitherto been divided into two categories – Class 6a for those built specially for trials (cars such as the Dellow, and many 'one-day trial' specials which have been road-equipped); and 6b for non-production cars such as the Buckler and re-engined Ford Populars which, although standing a better chance than the cars in the production-based classes with only limited modifications, were still no match for the cars in 6a. But the VW-based Buggies and other hybrids have spoiled all this as they qualify for 6b – yet can climb better than a Dellow!

The decision to change the classes was not an easy one – and indeed, a few years ago, led to a revolt among members which, without very careful handling, might well have split the Club; and, even now, any suggestion that a particular hill is to be 'made easier' results in a spate of letters complaining bitterly about the proposed alterations. The 1988 rules were, however, the result of much negotiation between the MCC, the Association of Classic Trials Clubs (of which the MCC is a leading member), and the RAC Motor Sports

Association. And the MCC has sub-committees dealing separately with car and motor-cycle regulations, constantly monitoring what is happening and trying to remove the anomalies in the regulations before advantage can be taken of them. Doctoring – to a degree – of some hills is necessary if the classic hills are to be kept in use. New hills are getting progressively more difficult to find, and members like to feel they are using the same hills year after year, so that the challenge remains the same – in contrast with motor-car and motor-cycle racing where circuits are altered each year to suit the increasing speeds and the developing ideas of what makes a 'safe' circuit. So far as doctoring by local people is concerned – which is never malicious – on one or two occasions a hill that has been over-doctored has been omitted from the route for a year or two – which has usually brought appeals from the locals to reinstate it, followed by several years of non-doctoring!

The value of separate classes is that it allows the whole entry to tackle the whole route, using all the hills – with specific types of motor-cycles and cars being set a slightly different task on each hill, in keeping with their own expected climbing power. Occasionally a particular hill may be limited to cars or to motor-cycles, or even to certain categories, but this is avoided if possible because competitors like to feel they are all attempting the same obstacles, and that their 'First' (if they win one) is worth as much as anybody else's.

As a general rule, in the previous regulations, Classes a, b, d, 1, 2, 3 and 4 were put into Category A, while Classes c, 5 and 6 were in Category B with extra re-starts and different tests (see Appendix 4 for the 1988 regulations). There may also have been separate re-start lines for Classes 6a and 6b, although, as mentioned earlier, modern design and adaptation made a bit of a mockery of the regulations in force until the end of the 1987 programme.

The underlying principle throughout the MCC's long history has been that a well-handled, sensibly-prepared ordinary car can acquit itself well – and it looks as though the propositions put forward by the late Squadron Leader A. F. Scroggs at the 1954 AGM may have done much to keep this principle in line with the greater versatility of today's motor-cycles and cars.

With the fiftieth Anniversary 'retrospective' *Edinburgh* taking place on 21–22 May, the 1954 Edinburgh Rally became the Whitsun Rally on 4–5 June, for which there were 128 entries – 52 solos, 3 sidecars, one three-wheeler and 72 cars. The event converged on Harrogate as usual, from the various starting points, followed by a 285-mile route in the Pennines, the Westmorland area of the Lake District, including Park Rash, Oughtershaw Side, and Hardknott, Wrynose, Kirkstone and Buttertubs passes. This was punctuated by a series of special tests, of which Park Rash did not please many. An undulating section on rising ground had to be covered flat-out, followed by a similar section to be taken dead slow – with disastrous effects on clutches. There was a consistency test on Hardknott (two sections to be taken at identical speeds); a downhill brake test on Wrynose; a stop-and-re-start on Kirkstone; and a stop-and-re-start on Buttertubs, finishing with a very steep climb that made speed adjustment difficult. This – understandably – was unpopular among the motor-cycle entry, many of whom had no stopwatch; and those who had were scarcely in a position to use them.

The Committee agreed that working out the results of these tests had become extremely difficult and involved far too many calculations. A decision was eventually taken that the results committee should commit themselves only to the figure-of-merit for the whole Rally! This, in turn, did not make the Stewards' job too easy when it came to dealing with protests. All in all, it seems to have been a somewhat contentious event.

With the National Rally now sponsored by Redex (see Chapter 8), and as ever taking up so much time, particularly at the expense of the motor-cycle members, it was first proposed that the Autumn Trial on 9 October should

1972: Tom Threlfall, past VSCC President and current editor of the MCC's journal *Triple*, is a regular competitor in the classic trials in his sedate and extremely successful Ford Model A Tudor saloon.

1972: After usually appearing in non-competitive cars, ex-racing driver John Aley found the *Land's End* almost too easy in his specially built 'big'-engined Volkswagen – as did his passenger, who listens to the Boat Race commentary on the car radio!

be abandoned. During lengthy discussions it was suggested that the Club was placing altogether too much emphasis on the National Rally – this line of attack being halted abruptly when it was pointed out that the 1953 event had brought in 59 new members! A sub-committee was formed to decide what sort of event should be run on 9 October, with the proviso 'that, in the organisation of this event, as little work as possible should fall on the office staff'. An Autumn Touring Trial was agreed, with the start and finish at the Evenlode Hotel, Eynsham and including non-stop sections and special tests. A route of 146 miles was laid out and the entry was small, totalling around 150 motor-cycles and cars.

The regulations were, as usual, sent to the RAC and ACU for approval but the latter took so long to reply that the regulations had been printed by the time their letter arrived. Although their eight suggested amendments were of a very trivial nature, they were adopted rather than cause ill-feeling with the ACU. Following the event, which most people said they had enjoyed, there were six complaints about the form in which the trial had been run, the writers demanding the return of their entry fees. So upset was the Chairman, who had spent much time organising and running the event, that he offered

Hardy annual: Operated by several generations of the Carlyon family, this venerable motor winch has assisted thousands of competitors to the summit of Bluehills Mine in the Land's End Trial – its drum by chance being geared to precisely the right speed.

his resignation. The solution adopted was to return the entry fees – but this incident illustrates the sort of disappointments that are faced by organising committees, about which the vast majority of happy, satisfied competitors know absolutely nothing.

For the main Committee, 1954 had not been without its problems; and adding to them was the fact that a forgetful or tight-fisted total of 578 members had failed to pay their 1953 and 1954 subscriptions, in contrast with 845 fully paid-up.

The relationship between the Main Committee and the various sub-committees was discussed at the close of the year, Major Marians putting forward a set of proposals which were adopted:

a. That the Main Committee should be referred to by its proper title, the Executive Committee.
b. That the following sub-committees should be appointed before the close of 1954, to act for 1955:
Finance and General Purposes
Social and Awards
Land's End Trial

Whitsun Rally (Edinburgh)
Race Meeting
Inter-Club Team Trial
Autumn Trial
National Motor Rally
Exeter Trial

Each of these was to be pretty well autonomous with its own Chairman, who would submit reports to the Executive Committee; they, in turn, undertook to accept such reports with a minimum of discussion unless vital points were involved – and providing, of course, that regulations were drawn up in accordance with the Club's accepted style and requirements. A schedule of dates for each sub-committee was to be submitted to them by the Secretary, advising them when the following items should be received in the office for subsequent action: draft of regulations; draft of route; dates by which the sub-committee must pass proofs of regulations and route cards, and any other items submitted to them. This arrangement successfully tied-up a number of increasingly loose ends, and it has worked well.

The fixture list for 1955 was drawn up, along with the dates for which the Secretary was authorised to apply: Land's End Trial (8–9 April), Whitsun Rally (27–28 May), Race Meeting (2 July; open to all types of machine, including racing), Inter-Club Team Trial (23 July), Autumn Trial (8 October), National Motor Rally (9–12 November) and Exeter Trial (6–7 January 1956). By now the annual programme had become stable – though the National Motor Rally and Inter-Club Team Trial were not to survive for much longer (see Chapters 8 and 10).

For 1955 and subsequently the RAC issued an amplification of their regulations governing the eligibility of vehicles. Manufacturers' modifications were to be permitted to cars in Categories 1 and 4 (see Appendix 4) even if they were not included among the modifications listed in the regulations – provided that such modifications were catalogued or listed by the manufacturers and were on sale to the public in the ordinary way – and the number of such modifications sold corresponded to the required number of cars sold in each Category (500 in Category 1 and 25 in Category 4).

The *Exeter* traditionally opened the MCC year on 7–8 January. As originally scheduled for 31 December 1954 and 1 January 1955 it would also have closed 1954 for the Club, but the change was made in deference to members' wishes – and the anticipated accommodation problems with so many people likely to celebrate the occasion away from home. At 297 (138 solos, 23 sidecars, 3 three-wheelers and 133 cars) the total was five down on 1954 though the

1987: This picture, taken on the first part of Bluehills Mine, could equally well have been taken at any time during the past fifty years. It shows Barry Clarke's 1928 Austin Seven, a regular MCC and VSCC competitor, winner of the pre-1941 class in this event.

division of entries was roughly the same. Special conditions were set for the unforgiving and difficult Simms, with the best twenty-five per cent of assaults being conceded 'clean climbs' – whatever their actual performances on the hill. This must have proved something of a rod-in-pickle for the results committee who had to compare performances differing perhaps only by inches!

The 1950s brought the major decision to move the finish of the Land's End Trial from its traditional Land's End to Newquay. Difficulty in finding accommodation in the Land's End area for the large number of people involved is generally accepted as the reason for the move. In fact it was prompted more by a general disinterest in the event by the Penzance authorities – due, perhaps, to a lack of knowledge among a younger, post-war generation of town councillors of the traditions and renown of this annual event. When the decision was announced, the Penzance council sent a deputation to London to try and persuade the Committee to reverse their decision. There were even hints of an injunction to stop the title 'Land's End', but the Committee stood fast, and eventually parted on good terms. Nowadays there is a strong move for a return to Land's End, and the Penzance authorities are offering every possible assistance and encouragement.

While the *Exeter* and *Land's End* trials have retained their old popularity throughout the post-World War II years, with a steadily increasing car entry and a fairly static number of motor-cycles, it has been the *Edinburgh* that brought problems – not the least of which has been its lack of appeal to members, especially when run as a rally; at heart, MCC members are not rally enthusiasts. As mentioned earlier, there had been a tremendous proliferation of sporting events of all types in the immediate post-war years, in response to an extraordinary upsurge of enthusiasm. The popular rallying areas became saturated weekend after weekend, with a mass of motor clubs each trying to satisfy this demand.

Inevitably the Government stepped in, and in the mid-fifties it was agreed between the Ministry of Transport and the RAC (as Britain's governing body of motor sport) that the number of events run by each club should be rationed

One dab of the foot and that elusive First-Class Award is lost for another year! Dick Peachey's face says it all as his feet scrabble to maintain balance on Bluehill's slippery upper slopes.

– with the allocation of permits based upon the number of events already run by each club.

The MCC had no difficulty in obtaining permits for its long-established *Exeter* and *Land's End*, and for its Silverstone race meeting, motor-cycles-only Inter-Club Trial (first held in 1904), and Derbyshire Trial (first held as the Sporting Trial in 1925, becoming the Derbyshire in 1955) – especially the two off-road events that did not worry anyone. So far as the *Edinburgh* was concerned, the RAC were reluctant to accept it as a rally – or even as a trial – when run in the over-worked Derbyshire area; and the MCC were not all that anxious to continue running an event that was steadily losing in popularity and consequence. But, with its long history and status, the RAC could scarcely turn down the MCC's application for a third long-distance event, and a permit was granted.

In 1957, and for the next ten years until 1967, this odd-man-out became 'The Edinburgh and The Esso Scoot to Scotland', catering for the growing interest in scooters and small three-wheeled cars (Messerschmitt, Vespa and others). Except for the bewildering profusion of starting points (London, Abingdon, Kenilworth, Shardlow, Bristol, Leeds, Edinburgh, Manchester and Newcastle-upon-Tyne in 1959), the event retained its long-distance character, using much of the old route covered by the inter-war *Edinburgh* trials. The difficult sections, with their rough, stony surfaces and rock outcrops had by then been properly surfaced and presented no problems, even to the scooters. The first of these events was held on 2 and 3 August 1957 with an entry of exactly 100.

Subsequent events reverted to the traditional Whitsun weekend and, so long as the interest in scooters and miniature three-wheelers survived, the event was well supported. Including the normal, though small, entry of cars and motor-cycles taking part in what was variously termed the Edinburgh 'Trial' and 'Run', the entry increased from 100 in 1957 to 303 in 1959; after that, entries steadily declined, with 177 in 1964, 102 in 1966 and only 85 in 1967, the last year it was held. Since then the 'road sections' of the *Edinburgh* (which means the overnight run from the start to the trials section) have been run as a 'Touring Assembly'. In effect, this means that the MCC avoids paying the RAC a high permit fee for what is no longer an entry-puller, while still retaining the traditional title of what has become the world's oldest-established long-distance event for motor-cycles.

Today's *Edinburgh* starts near Coventry, running through the night on main roads to Derbyshire, where the trial proper begins, the first motor-cycle entry leaving the start at around 8pm on the Friday. Including the overnight route from the start, the total distance covered is not far short of that of the

Exeter, and the number of observed sections tackled by competitors during the Saturday is also comparable with the *Exeter*.

In the intervening years the MCC's annual calendar has been whittled down to the four long-standing events for which the Club has become famous – the three classic trials and the Silverstone race meetings, and even that is now for motor-cycles only (see Chapter 9). Through the years it has been a case of the MCC providing outlets for members' specific enthusiasms – and then opting out of them when other clubs had taken them up in strength and the MCC's contributions were no longer necessary. This was particularly so with rallies during the early post-World War II years. Although the MCC is sometimes dubbed a 'fuddy-duddy' organisation, living largely in the past, it has throughout the years pioneered specific types of event and, having got a particular line started, abandoned it – except where the events remain unique.

In retrospect, the 'downs' in the Club's history have often coincided with the 'ups' in the general sporting scene. One suspects that the present wave-crest upon which the MCC is riding, with its steadily growing membership and over-subscribed entry-lists, stems from an overall feeling that the sport as a whole is becoming too professional, while the Club still continues to cater steadfastly for people who prefer to place their emphasis upon the word 'sport'.

CHAPTER 8

Daily Express, Redex and Hastings Rallies

With the car entry in the three classic trials having long outstripped the motor-cycle, people were beginning to suggest that the title 'Motor Cycling Club' was becoming something of a misnomer – that the 'Motor Car Club' might be more appropriate. These feelings were much in the minds of the Committee when, petrol rationing having been lifted in 1950, it was proposed to run a major, long-distance, cars-only rally. Acutely aware of the original motives behind the formation of the MCC almost half a century before, and of their true allegiance, the Committee proposed to run a similar event for motor-cycles. However, by a stroke of luck, the Scarborough MCC were planning to run precisely such an event during 1950, and it was agreed unanimously to use this as a test-case before going ahead with their own event. Clearly indicating the feelings among motor-cyclists, the proposed Scarborough Rally attracted only 31 entries and the event was scrapped, leaving the Committee with clear consciences.

It was at the February 1950 Committee meeting that R. C. (Bob) Porter first proposed the idea of the car rally; subsequently, his suggestion developed into thoughts of a full-scale, 1,000-mile event run under an International permit in connection with the Festival of Britain at Whitsuntide 1951. Approaches were made to Col Stanley Barnes, Manager of the Competitions Department of the RAC (and himself a regular competitor in MCC trials between the wars), who refused to grant an International permit as the RAC were themselves planning to run a similar event at the same time.

In the meantime, the MCC's General Secretary, Jackie Masters, had been in contact with *The Daily Express*, who also had in mind sponsoring a long-distance car rally – but in their case to be held before the end of 1950, and to be run under a National permit (which meant, in effect, that competitors must hold a National British competition licence, as distinct from an International). Further lengthy discussions were held with the RAC Competitions Department regarding the title of the event, and the type of permit under which it should be run. It was only after Tom Blackburne (Director and General Manager) and Albert Asher (P. R. Manager) – both of *The Daily Express* – had discussed the matter with Wilfrid Andrews (Chairman of the RAC) that agreement was reached – that the event should be called the 'MCC/*Daily Express* Rally', and that it should be run under a National permit; furthermore, that it should be run before the end of 1950! Even this was not the end of the deliberations, the club and the newspaper finally settling to run the event under a Restricted permit and to call it '*The Daily Express* Rally'.

From the original concept of a fully international event, run under an International permit in 1951 with foreign drivers and teams taking part, the status was reduced to a Restricted permit – with the event to be run in 1950. Time was incredibly short, though this never seems to have worried the MCC much (vide the 1910 Exeter Trial, which was conceived, planned and run in a matter of weeks).

During July 1950 an organising committee was set up, consisting of Basil Clark, Leslie Freeman, Vicky Gardner, Bob Porter and the Secretary of the Rally Jackie Masters (for more about this outstanding MCC official, see Chapter 12). It was estimated that the event could be run for around £2,000 and *The Daily Express* undertook to provide the publicity, printing and awards. Under the Restricted permit, the following clubs were invited to compete: Scottish Sporting CC, Brighton and Hove MC, BARC, Lancashire AC, Yorkshire Sporting CC, and SUNBAC. Non-members of the MCC were to be given provisional membership for 10 shillings (50p), which covered the subscription for the remainder of the year, and entry fees were set at £4 with an additional team entry fee of £1.

Temporary staff were taken on for the intensely busy nineteen week period ahead, plus an extra typist as there was more work than even Mrs Harris, the MCC's long-suffering and popular permanent secretary could manage; and J. D. Ferguson, of Andrew Barr and Co, was appointed to handle the results on a professional basis with the help of two of his staff.

Seven starting controls were chosen: Plymouth, Norwich, Leamington

The MCC has always catered for all tastes and there can be few bigger contrasts than these two cars with consecutive numbers in the 1952 National Rally. The Jupiter takes a tight line into the 'Box' at the finish of a special test while C. R. E. Edsall's little Ford Eight Estate looks almost lost on a Lakeland pass.

Spa, London, Manchester, Harrogate and Glasgow. All seven groups of competitors were to converge on Chester after a run of 750 miles apiece. The 350-mile common route from Chester to the finish at Torquay was laid out through Mold, Ruthin, Cerrig-y-Druidon, Frongoch, Bala, Dolgelly and Dinas Mawddy to the summit of Bwylch-y-Groes – and on through Llanfan, Caereinion, Llangadfan, Bettws-Cedewain, Newton and Knighton to Ross-on-Wye and Gloucester. From here the route was to take familiar MCC territory in the south-west – Minehead, Lynmouth and Blackmoor Gate down to the finish at Torquay where the final Eliminating Tests were to be held (braking, acceleration and parking – popular rally gimmicks of the day).

Arthur Bourne (editor of *The Motor Cycle*) was appointed to organise the Welsh route, with help from H. P. Baugham, siting control points, meal halts and so on; and Professor A. M. Low and Major Lewis undertook to produce a class-equalising formula for the rolling braking test on Shedden Hill. As most of the tricky Welsh section was to be covered in darkness, Basil de Mattos (today's MCC President) and Ken Roberts surveyed it by night in a side-valve Morris Minor loaned by Morris Motors, confirming that the required 24.5mph

average speed, including all stops, was within the capabilities of all engine capacity classes.

In addition to this formidable amount of work and planning, there were the arrangements with the Torquay authorities who agreed to set aside space for parking, for the final tests, and for the Concours d'Elegance on the day following the finish – which meant closing the sea front for three hours; they also undertook to provide accommodation and food for a sudden influx of up to 1,000 people.

So far as the competitors were concerned, marks were to be deducted for late starting, and for late or early arrival at any control. From the seven starting points to Chester, an allowance of fifteen minutes late or early was permitted free of penalty; from Chester to Torquay this was reduced to five minutes early or fifteen late. Further marks could be lost in the timed Elimination Tests at the finish, and for bodywork damage; inoperative self-starters, horns and lamps; and damaged silencers.

It was planned that Plymouth should be the first of the starting controls, with the first car leaving at 10am on Wednesday 8 November 1950, followed by the others at one-minute intervals – Plymouth being followed by the remaining six starting points in succession. The first car from Plymouth was due at the Torquay finish at 7.30am on Friday November 10. Apart from £500 in cash prizes, there were the *Daily Express* trophies for the outright winner, class winners, best placed car from each starting point, and the best placed team of three cars. The Concours d'Elegance was to be an entirely separate contest, judged solely on beauty of external lines, and cleanliness of bodywork inside and out. The entries were divided up according to their year of manufacture. Rally officials were L. A. Baddeley (MCC President), Dudley Noble and Geoffrey Smith as Stewards; J. C. (Bob) Lowe as Chief Timekeeper; and Jackie Masters as Clerk of the Course and Secretary of the Meeting.

Thankful no doubt for this sudden boost to the town's trade during the tourist off-season, the Mayor of Torquay planned to welcome competitors, officials and the Press at a cocktail party on the evening of the finish. On the following day, after the Concours d'Elegance, there was to be a Gala Rally Dinner and Ball, including the prize-giving at Torquay's Grand Hotel.

Considering that the decision to go ahead was not taken until June/July, the organisation of this major event was a remarkable achievement, which could have been undertaken only at a time when the country was starved of motor sporting events, of which there were still relatively few to be co-ordinated. The first Press announcements of the rally were made in August, and the regulations were distributed on 29 September. Within a very few days no fewer than 800-plus entries had been received – for an event with an entry limited to 400! Because of this large and popular response, the RAC extended the permit to 450.

Among the accepted entries were 15 Allards, 48 MGs, 21 Rileys, 36 Austins, 9 HRGs, 34 Fords, 22 Jowetts and 17 Jaguars. The 1950 Monte Carlo Rally winners, Marcel Becquart and Henri Secret entered a Hotchkiss and were allocated the number 121, but because they could not take part without a British competition licence they followed the event around as an also-ran – until the engine blew up.

Bob Porter's $2^1/_2$-litre Riley was first away from the Plymouth start, heading the large column of 450 cars as they travelled along their eight separate routes to converge on Chester. These included, in the Vintage class, a 1923 3-litre Bentley, and a $4^1/_2$-litre '100mph' Invicta driven by film cameraman Peter Hennessy and John Tucker-Peake (past editor of the MCC's journal *Triple*). There were few problems along the converging routes, but the Welsh section, driven in darkness, produced havoc, many competitors losing their way despite the clear instructions on the route cards provided. Conditions on Bwylch-y-Groes were extremely bad, with visibility down almost to nil after the infamous hairpin. Cars were baulked by others which had stopped with burnt-out clutches, overheated engines, punctured fuel tanks – and, in a few cases, sheer lack of power. The few main road stretches included in the Welsh section provided little opportunity for making up time, and there was no question of resting at controls; it was in . . .sign on . . .and away at once. As a result, many were penalised for lateness.

In the final tests at Torquay the majority lost a few marks on the braking test, though only 37 lost the maximum; all lost marks on the acceleration tests; and on the parking tests all but forty or so incurred the maximum penalty marks. With today's major rallies won or lost entirely on the road (whether 'the road' means forestry stages, mountain passes or whatever), the possibility of losing marks in a few driving tests after a penalty-free, 1,100-mile drive including some extremely demanding conditions seems altogether wrong. But that was the way of rallies in those early post-war years, including such as the Monte Carlo. The principal justification for this practice was that the tests provided entertainment for large numbers of spectators – otherwise rally drivers went about their sport pretty well unobserved in remote places, and usually in darkness.

Overall winners were Geoff Holt (a top trials driver at the time) and Stan Asbury in a 1,250cc MG TD Midget, with Ian and Jean Appleyard second in a Jaguar XK120, and Len Shaw and Doug Lawton third (1,250cc MG saloon). (For full results of this series of events, see Appendix 5).

Organisation of the second 'Daily Express' was basically the same as in 1950, but with the rally headquarters and finishing control at Hastings instead of Torquay. The organising committee consisted of F. W. J. Bolton, A. C. Cookson, R. W. Clarke, and Basil de Mattos who took charge of the Welsh section. The event was run under full National permit, with a maximum of 450 entries, and was more than handsomely over-subscribed, thanks largely to the success of the 1950 event.

As before, the Plymouth starters left first, headed by the first car at 8am on Wednesday 7 November, followed at one-minute intervals by the rest of the Plymouth starters, and then successively by those from Manchester, Leamington Spa, Norwich, Cardiff, Glasgow, London and Harrogate. All eight groups converged on Penrith this time, instead of Carlisle, before embarking on the common route. Regularity Tests were included on Newlands Hause and Honister Pass; and the usual Eliminating Tests were laid on at Hastings following the end of the road section.

Among the 450 entries there were 69 MGs, 36 Jaguars, 25 Rileys, 24 Jowetts and 13 HRGs, with separate classes for supercharged cars, non-production cars, and trials specials. The entry list included several drivers who in later years were to become household names in big-time, international rallying – Sheila Van Damm, Nancy Mitchell, Joy Cooke,

1952: KUY 474 driven by Jacky Ray in the National rally. The car was later to appear as the regular trials' mount of Tom Threlfall.

Jackie and Peter Reece and others. The cars varied from supercharged trials specials, via Vintage and sports cars to everyday family saloons. 'Doc' and Mrs Lilley drove their 1,172cc Clegg Special which, three weeks before, had been battling with the High Peaks Trial and, a week later, was mud-plugging in the Gloster. Ken Rawlings drove his well-known Standard Vanguard-engined trials car 'Buttercup' and was fastest in most of the tests.

The event was run in a downpour with heavy flooding on the Welsh section causing many delays, and further flooding on the Presteigne, Hay-on-Wye, and Ewyas Harold route. When the results were published it was clear someone had made a serious error in timing the Regularity Tests. A meeting of the Stewards was hurriedly called – Stanley Barnes of the RAC, L. A. Baddeley, F. A. Applebee, Dudley Noble and J. M. Toulmin – who established that a timekeeper's stop-watch had stopped and been re-started without synchronisation. The Newlands Hause and Honister Pass Tests were therefore cancelled.

Again, the event was won by a 1,250cc MG TD Midget (R. A. Hopkinson and Mrs Hopkinson), with J. V. S. Brown and R. W. Kettel second in an HRG, and Ken Rawlings and L. J. Tracey third in Rawlings' Vanguard

Special, 'Buttercup'. The first three finishers in the Ladies' Awards were Joy Cooke (1,172cc Ford), Nancy Mitchell (1,496cc HRG) and Sheila Van Damm (2,267cc Sunbeam-Talbot). The well known motor-cyclist Bob Foster – who had emerged the overall winner before the Regularity Test miscalculations had been sorted out – was given a special consolation prize of £50, which was greeted with heartfelt cheers at the prize-giving dinner.

Such was the growth in enthusiasm for motor sport following the war years that, whereas 660 permits were issued by the RAC for events held in 1952, 138 of them speed events, these figures had soared to 4,000-plus and 250 respectively by the early 1980s – with an astonishing 10,000 or so waivers of permit.

The general format of the 1952 event, third in the series, was very much the same as for the previous two years. The same eight starting points were used, with the 450 starters converging on Penrith for the second year before embarking on the more difficult and slightly altered common route through Wales. Continuing to ring the changes for the rally headquarters and finishing control, and having given Torquay and Hastings a turn, the organising committee moved along the coast to Brighton, where the end-of-rally Eliminating Tests and Concours d'Elegance were held the following day on Madeira Drive.

Among the 'names' this time was Stirling Moss in a Jaguar XK120, with *The Autocar*'s John Cooper as co-driver. After a relatively easy, fine weather road section on which few of the more skilled drivers lost marks, the final Eliminating Tests assumed even greater importance this year, virtually deciding the results – and it was again the small, nimble open cars that starred, being ideally suited to these tests. The event was won outright by 'Doc' and Mrs Hardman in a supercharged Dellow, with Ken Rawlings' Vanguard Special now up in second place and W. A. G. Goodall's Morgan third.

A somewhat critical letter appeared in *The Autocar* complaining that the first 20 placings in the overall results had been taken by open cars; that saloons didn't stand a chance, and that there should be separate classifications for open and closed cars. This was only partly true, however, as a Morgan running throughout with a hood up, as a closed car, driven by Peter and Mrs Morgan finished fourth, with Stirling Moss's fixed-head Jaguar 14th, and a Vauxhall saloon (Turnbull and Harper) 16th. Perhaps even more significant was that the drivers who were regularly doing well in the MCC classic – and other – trials were also featuring high in the rally results, suggesting that it was the drivers, as much as their cars, that mattered.

The 1953 event was the last to be run under *Daily Express* sponsorship. There were seven starting controls – Plymouth, Manchester, Kenilworth, Norwich, London, Cardiff and Glasgow. All seven routes converged on Harrogate after some 360 miles. From Harrogate to the finish – back again at Hastings – competitors followed a common route through the Yorkshire, Westmorland and Cumberland moors to the Scottish Lowlands and down through Wales to the finish. The total road section covered 1,230 miles and, as usual, included no 'trials sections' or chassis-breakers. Various tests were included along the route, with the final Eliminating Tests at the finish.

A standard average speed was set for each engine capacity class, and the winner of the event was the competitor who exceeded by the greatest percentage the average 'ormance set up in his class. This was a new way of sorting out the winners, and it was intended to equalise the chances of all cars, whether powerful and fast or more mundane; the faster cars, for example, were set a more demanding schedule than the family saloons. The procession of nearly 450 cars took roughly $7\frac{1}{2}$ hours to pass through any given point. As before, the Plymouth contingent moved off first, starting at 8am on Wednesday 11 November 1953, and finishing at 8am on Friday 13 November with the Eliminating Tests on the same day and the Concours d'Elegance on the Saturday.

With weather conditions worse than in any of its predecessors, the event was by far the toughest, with a high percentage of retirements and penalisations compared with previous years. The new method of marking brought its anomalies for, although Ken Rawlings and Lou Tracey in the ubiquitous Vanguard Special 'Buttercup' lost fewest marks overall, the winner was Frank Grounds with co-driver W. H. Bartley in a Sunbeam-Talbot saloon. In fact, the first four cars in the overall classification were in the same class. Second, third and fourth were R. K. N. Clarkson and C. C. Wells in a special-bodied Morgan coupé, H. C. and Mrs Roberts in a Ford Zephyr, and Nancy Mitchell and Pat Faichney in another Zephyr. It was to avoid this situation that the new marking system had been devised. If the results had been based, as previously, on the number of penalty marks incurred regardless of class, the first four finishers would have come from four different classes.

There were other criticisms among competitors. Too much emphasis they felt had been placed upon the 20-mile Regularity Test laid out along the road section through Yorkshire. The required average speed was not disclosed until the start of the test, and there were secret checks along the 20 miles. Precisely consistent progress depended upon odometers, notoriously inaccurate in their readings, and cross-checks on map landmarks – a pretty hit-or-miss set-up by any standards; and the marking was such that even a small error could put a competitor out of the running.

As *The Autocar* commented: 'These, while all minor points, are the sort of avoidable errors which should not be made by a club with the wealth of experience of the MCC.' Despite this, however, it was generally agreed to have been the toughest and most enjoyable *Daily Express* Rally in the series.

Redex, sponsors of the 9,600-mile Round Australia Trial at the time, took over from *The Daily Express* as sponsors of the 1954 event, held from 10 to 13 November. For the first time since the rally was inaugurated, with its 800-plus applications for 450 entries, the numbers were substantially down with 334 cars setting out from the usual seven starting controls on the 359-mile converging routes to Harrogate. Thence the combined route led north to Hawick, down through the Lake District to Chester, and into Wales with a test on Bwylch-y-Groes, and others along the route. This section was, as usual, covered during the night before heading back into 'civilisation' through Tewkesbury, Marlborough, Stockbridge, Battle and Hastings.

The much more demanding Welsh section was made stiffer still by continuous bad weather and, of the 334 starters (out of 385 entries), 82 retired along the route and a further 45 were excluded for being outside the maximum permitted time limits. There were 207 classified finishers. The system of marking was basically the same as in the 1953 event, but this time the far tougher Welsh section, coupled with the weather, did more to sort out the winners, the tests assuming less significance.

Winners were E. R. Parsons and Mrs Vann in a Mark VII Jaguar – a big, family saloon which proved at last that success need not be confined to small, nimble sports cars. They lost no marks on the road section and incurred only 13.33 penalty marks in the tests, thereby exceeding the standard for their class by the greatest margin. It was a remarkable achievement in this, their second-ever rally. A. L. Yarranton and D. Thompson finished second in a Morgan Plus Four, having also completed the road section 'clean', and scored only 10.27 penalty marks – fewer than any other competitor. This again showed up the anomalies in the marking system, but in view of the disparity between the two cars, the big Jaguar's was an extremely popular win.

There was no actual sponsor for the 1955 event, though *The Autocar* put up a trophy and cheque for £100 for the outright winner; and it was re-named the MCC Hastings Rally. Entry fees were increased from six to eight guineas, which may have been a contributing factor in the further reduction of entries to 222. Another influence may have been the fact that, when the regulations were first published, Production Touring cars (Category 1) were grouped with Grand Touring cars (Category 2), which meant that the more mundane family saloons were competing on level terms with the much more sporting Grand Tourers. This was later altered; Category 2 cars were combined with Category 3 (Modified Touring cars), which was much fairer. Those people deterred by the original groupings may very well have failed to spot the change before entries had closed.

Of the 222 entries, there were 26 non-starters, bringing the field down to below 200. The route was very much the same as in previous years, except that the Westcountry, Plymouth starting control had been replaced by Taunton; by far the greater number of competitors chose the London start. Though, in keeping with their policy, the MCC avoided any chassis-breaking sections along the Welsh route, some of the sections, taken again at night, were extremely rough; and there were the usual tests along the route, in addition to those at Hastings after the finish.

Of the 196 starters, 66 failed to reach the finish; and of the 130 that did so, 51 had been penalised on the road section and ten lost marks for bodywork damage.

Once again an MG Midget won the event outright – the third in six events – this time a pre-war TA driven by S. P. A. Freeman and L. C. Eversden, a car which Freeman had owned for 16 years, and had chosen for the event in preference to his XK Jaguar.

It is not difficult to understand why the popularity of this event was steadily decreasing, though it was well organised and thoroughly enjoyed by most of those who took part. 'The MCC Rally was a great success from every-body's point of view . . .' *The Autocar* reported in 1955. There was, however, an increasing feeling among the more serious competitors that rallies should be 'won on the road'. What was the point, they wondered, of covering long distances, often in tough, demanding conditions, without loss of marks – only to be ruled out by some minor error in an insignificant driving test after the finish? This point of view was emphasised by the fact that, by 1955, pretty well all the topmost 'names' in the sport of rallying had vanished from the entry lists. It was not until the off-road Forestry Commission stages came into being – and before them the use of the less appropriate racing circuits – that these principles could be applied and the driving tests abandoned.

The entry list was further reduced to 172 for the 1956 event, of which only 151 set out from the same seven starting controls used in 1955. The 1,200-mile route was almost the same, though with additional tests, includ-ing a six-mile navigation test soon after the Harrogate converging point. There was no penalty for early arrival at Harrogate (or at any other control). Route cards for the navigation section were handed out immediately upon arrival at Harrogate, giving the crews plenty of time to become thoroughly familiar with the intricacies of the test. This was proved to be a mistake; what could have been a difficult test was made easy – for all but the thoroughly inexperienced. Toughest section was the Hirnant Pass, in Wales, which was deep in mud, deeply cross-gullied and rock-strewn. Many less skilled drivers were brought to a standstill and there were considerable delays. The stewards agreed to drop this section and cancel the penalty points incurred – but there were so many protests from the experienced drivers who had climbed the pass successfully that the section was reinstated. Only 99 cars emerged from the difficult night in Wales to check in at Tewkesbury.

This time the marking system worked well, with the outright winner R. W. Dalglish (Triumph TR2) actually scoring fewer penalty marks than any other competitor. According to contemporary reports, this was 'by far the toughest event in the series', a statement that seems to have been made successively year by year since the MCC Rally was first held. But, as the experts claimed, it was still not tough enough for them. I wrote in *The Autocar* at the time: 'This presents something of a problem for the MCC who, since the turn of the century, have maintained a policy of running events for everyday drivers of everyday cars; in the past the inherent unreliability of cars usually sorted things out over the longish distances involved. Unfortunately, however, modern cars are so dependable and experienced rally crews so numerous that unless an event is thoroughly sporting and pretty tough its appeal to the experts will be lost and the entries fall off.'

This was what was happening. It was clearly no longer possible for the MCC to play this unsuccessful 'best of both worlds' role. Though dates were applied for, and the usual RAC National permit was granted for the 1957 event, the MCC issued the following statement in August 1957:

After careful consideration, the Committee have come to the conclusion that it would not be an economic proposition to run the event on the usual scale.

Rather than depart from the MCC standard of organisation, they have, therefore, regretfully decided to cancel the event for 1957.

CHAPTER 9

Brooklands to Silverstone

To locate them in the general order of things during the club's formative years, brief mention was made in Chapter 2 of the first speed events for motor-cycles run by the MCC on the old Brooklands track. Built by Hugh Fortescue Locke-King on part of his estate near Weybridge, and named after his home 'Brooklands House', this immensely ambitious and much-loved 'Motor Course' was a bare twenty-five miles to the south-west of London.

In 1989, it is 50 years since the track last heard the sound of racing cars, and of motor-cycles, doing battle – longer by far than the thirty-two years during which it was in constant use. And only those maybe in their sixties, and older, can recall first-hand the great, white Outer Circuit – always, in the memory, blessed by brilliant sunshine; and the provocative smell of burned Castrol R which hung in the air on still days and which, for some reason, was pleasant even to people with no interest in motor racing or aviation. To those of us old enough to have known its magic, the loss of Brooklands was (and still is) a disaster – as it was to Britains' motor industry, although their needs have now been met by the proving ground near Nuneaton.

Locke-King's far-sightedness, patriotism and initiative in building the track were remarkable. In October 1906, when the task of clearing the acres of swampy wasteland began, British cars had been conspicuously absent from such as the French GP (first held in 1906) and the Targa Florio of that year, at which Locke-King had been a spectator and from which much of his inspiration must have arisen. It took only eight months from when the work began until the 2 miles, 1,350 yards of the pear-shaped Outer Circuit were complete and ready for racing, with the high Byfleet and Home (or Members') bankings at opposite ends of the 'pear', each designed for 'hands-off' speeds of 120mph. The Mountain and Campbell circuits came much later, in 1930 and 1937 respectively, the latter a simulated 'road circuit'.

The opening race meeting was held on 6 July 1907; and the steadily growing annual programme of meetings was joined by the MCC on Saturday, 16 October 1909 with a meeting which was held annually at Brooklands, with a break for World War I, until 1939, when the tearing-apart of the old 'Motor Course' began.

That this first meeting should have been for motor-cycles only was not surprising; it was in keeping with the early events in the Edinburgh and Land's End series of trials. And that it should have been an out-and-out race meeting was to be expected, in view of the success of the club's original event at the Crystal Palace in 1902 – regarded as the first motor-cycle race meeting ever to be held in this country. And Brooklands was the obvious choice in view of their experience of events in this category ever since motor-cycles had first raced there on 18 April 1908. What is perhaps surprising is that it should have been necessary to open the meeting to non-members as well as to MCC members. It may have been feared, with the club's other events catering exclusively for touring machines, that the entry for a race meeting might have been disappointingly small if limited to members only – who were not racers and did not own racing machines. It was an event that was out of character with the club's avowed principle of catering for ordinary people with ordinary machines – and it was to continue out of character for many years to come.

The appropriate Minutes Book records nothing about the thinking behind the earliest Brooklands events – which can be forgiven because the first of these and the authorisation of the Hon Secretary to buy himself a typewriter occurred roughly simultaneously, after which the Minutes became brief, with little mention of anything. Then as now, brevity was the only substitute for lack of operating skill! Even the programme of events for 1909, drawn up at the 18 January 1909 Committee meeting, makes no mention of the Brooklands event held on 16 October the same year. Possibly it was another 'pierhead jump' like the first *Exeter*, and the first *Daily Express* Rally 41 years later (see Chapter 8).

With a break for World War I the Brooklands meetings continued in their motor-cycles only, open to non-members series of purely racing events until, in 1924, it was decided to change the format. It had long been felt that, instead of catering for the type of motor-cycles and cars used by members in the Club's long-distance road events, the meetings were being run for

The ...

MOTOR CYCLING CLUB LTD.

(Founded 1901)

Programme and Final Regulations

OF THE FIRST

100 Miles High Speed Reliability Run

AT

BROOKLANDS TRACK

WEYBRIDGE

OCTOBER 17th :: 1925

(Open to Members of the Motor Cycling Club only)

For Motor Cycles, Sidecars, Three-wheeled Cycle Cars and Cars of any horse-power
In accordance with the following Regulations

_____

Car Entries are subject to the Closed Competition Rules of the R.A.C., together with the following Regulations, which have been approved by the R.A.C.

_____

PRICE ONE SHILLING

Between 1925 and 1938 the growing influence of the designer can be seen in the covers of MCC programmes, although there was little he could do about the contents. The programme's cover-price halved during those years.

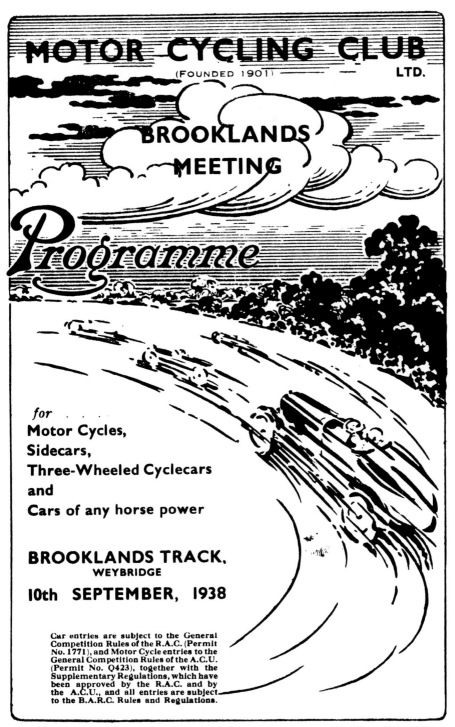

MOTOR CYCLING CLUB

(FOUNDED 1901)

LTD.

BROOKLANDS MEETING

Programme

for . . .

Motor Cycles,

Sidecars,

Three-Wheeled Cyclecars

and

Cars of any horse power

BROOKLANDS TRACK,
WEYBRIDGE

10th SEPTEMBER, 1938

Car entries are subject to the General Competition Rules of the R.A.C. (Permit No. 1771), and Motor Cycle entries to the General Competition Rules of the A.C.U. (Permit No. Q423), together with the Supplementary Regulations, which have been approved by the R.A.C. and by the A.C.U., and all entries are subject to the B.A.R.C. Rules and Regulations.

PRICE SIXPENCE

1925: A typical pit scene during the October Brooklands meeting. J. J. Boyd-Harvey (No 4, 348cc Douglas) appears to be re-starting, while an official checks W. H. Julien's 247cc Levis sidecar (No 34).

non-members with racing or specially prepared and stripped road machines – at the expense of members. It was hoped that by making changes the Club's activities so far as the ordinary members were concerned could be increased.

The rules were framed expressly to encourage this. Motor-cycles and cars had to be in full touring trim with mudguards and full road equipment, including lamps, horn, spare wheel, hood, windscreen and so on; in fact everything that the law required and that was fitted as original equipment by the manufacturer when the vehicle was new. Touring vehicles fitted with standard road exhaust systems could use them, but the addition of a Brooklands fish-tail was compulsory. Sporting vehicles that were not using the manufacturers' standard exhausts were obliged to fit a silencer complying with the Brooklands Regulation Silencer (see Appendix 2) specification.

Entries were restricted to MCC members, and anyone wishing to join and compete had to apply for membership at least three weeks before the event so as to allow time for their credentials to be checked. Each entrant had to provide his (there were no lady members as yet) own lap scorer, and each passenger in a passenger-carrying vehicle had to wear, for identification, a coloured jersey provided by the Club. Motor-cycle and three-wheeler entrants and passengers had to wear crash helmets – also provided by the Club. Intending competitors who had not previously ridden/driven on the track had to cover at least one lap under Brooklands official observation before taking part, and arrangements were made with the BARC whereby this could be done at any time during the week prior to the event. These rules came into effect in 1925.

The meetings mainly consisted of a run of one hour, the number of laps required to qualify for a First, Second or Third Class Award being laid down for each engine capacity class. In the early years a 250cc motor-cycle had to cover 15 laps (41.5 miles) and a car of unlimited capacity 22 laps (60.8 miles). These requirements were gradually increased in line with improving performances until the last-ever Brooklands meeting in 1938, when they were as follows:

One Hour Trial

Class	Capacity cc	Premier Award Laps	Premier Award Distance	Silver Medal Laps	Silver Medal Distance	Bronze Medal Laps	Bronze Medal Distance
Solo motor-cycles	250	23	63.63	20	55.34	17	49.80
	350	24	66.40	21	52.57	18	47.04
	500	25	69.16	22	60.87	19	52.57
	750	25	69.16	22	60.87	19	52.57
	Unlimited	25	69.16	22	60.87	20	53.54
Sidecars	350	18	49.80	15	41.50	13	35.96
	600	20	55.34	17	47.04	14	38.72
	Unlimited	22	60.87	19	52.57	16	44.27
Three-wheelers	Unlimited	23	63.63	20	55.34	17	47.64
Cars	850	22	60.87	19	52.57	16	44.27
	1,000	24	66.40	21	58.10	18	49.80
	1,500	27	74.68	24	66.40	21	58.10
	2,000	27	74.68	24	66.40	21	68.10
	Unlimited	29	80.20	26	71.92	23	63.63
Standard touring cars, open or closed	Up to 1,500	20	55.34	17	47.04	14	38.72
	Over 1,5000	23	63.63	20	55.34	17	47.64

These figures are as published in the Regulations. There is no explanation for the differing opinions as to the distance involved in completing twenty-one laps of the Outer Circuit, as expressed in the Silver Medal column (52.57 miles in line 2; 58.10 in line 11)! And it seems a little ambitious, in the solo motor-cycle classes that a 500cc ES2 Norton should have to cover as many miles in the hour as a 1,100cc Brough Superior Dream, or 998cc Vincent HRD twin. But that is how it was.

By now there were optional awards available for the winners of 'Premiers'. You could have a plated eight-day clock, engine-turned pewter cigarette box, silver-plated cigarette lighter or silver-plated tankard – all with a miniature medal insert. It was also possible to have all one's awards, including in the trials, held over for a composite award at the end of the season. The canteen of cutlery was popular.

Reverting to the 1920s, the major changes in the regulations, brought in for 1925, resulted in increasingly successful meetings as the years went by. Entries topped 240 in 1927, and the last Brooklands meeting, held in September 1938, produced 188. The smallest entry was in 1931, with 131; there were 203 in 1936 and 163 in 1937. These variations were possibly due to experimentation with the programme of events. For example, there were only three One-Hour Trials in 1934, plus a series of two-lap scratch races, and four one-lap races each for car classes up to and including 1,100cc, 1,300cc, 1,650cc and unlimited capacity. These were open only to certain makes: Race 1: Austin, Singer and MG Midgets. 2: MG Magna, Wolseley Hornet, Riley and Triumph. 3: Aston Martin, Alvis, Frazer Nash, Riley and Singer. 4: Lagonda, Railton, Hudson Terraplane, Ford and Talbot.

1927: The sun did not always shine on MCC events. Taken during a Brooklands One-Hour Trial, competitors pick their way past the famous Vickers sheds.

The development of cars and motor-cycles through the inter-war years can be clearly traced in the increasing distances covered – and therefore the speeds – in those One-Hour Trials. In 1927 the fastest motor-cycle was J. W. Beare's 500cc Zenith, which completed 23 laps (66.3mph); fastest Morgan three-wheeler was H. R. Taylor's with 25 laps (70mph); and fastest car was G. Fairrie's 1,990cc Bugatti with 29 laps (80.4mph).

A year later (1928), F. W. Clarke's little 250cc New Imperial averaged 65mph for the hour; W. Urquhart-Dykes' Alvis averaged 81.6; Brian Lewis (later Lord Essendon) averaged 85.5mph with his Talbot; and the two fastest motor-cycles, ridden by H. J. Bacon and H. W. Collier, both averaged 71.6mph. At the 1929 meeting, speeds rose considerably, with Max Aitken's $1^{1}/_{2}$-litre Aston Martin averaging 82.03mph and H. J. Aldington's Frazer Nash 83.84mph. In the larger car classes, Rex Mundy's 30/98 Vauxhall averaged 84.41mph and M. Durant's $4^{1}/_{2}$-litre Bentley 83.84mph. The fastest motor-cycles were T. F. Hall's 495cc Matchless and Steve Lancefield's 490cc Norton, with 84.61 and 80.13mph respectively. It was the motor-cycles that seem to have made the greatest advances in 1930, with H. P. Chantry's big 988cc Brough Superior understandably the fastest at 88.6mph, and H. J. Bacon's 493cc Sunbeam with 86.2mph. A. Kipling's 2,997cc Hotchkiss and Lord de Clifford's Lagonda recorded 84.41 and 84.27mph respectively.

Fastest motor-cycle in 1931 was Courtnay's 499cc Rudge, averaging 85.28mph – against Major A. T. Goldie Gardner's Rover Speed Tourer which, as fastest car, achieved 83.56mph. A number of two-lap scratch races were held for cars and motor-cycles – the winners of these competing in subsequent handicap events. The motor-cycle event was won by R. A. Macdermid, riding a 996cc Brough Superior, for which he received the Harry Smith Challenge Trophy (the 'Gold Cup'; see Chapter 2 for further details of this historic trophy). V. L. Seyd won the car event with his Austin 7 at 70.64mph for which he received the Albert Brown Challenge Trophy – to which there seem to be no further references in the Club's archives.

At the 1935 meeting Jock West, riding a BMW, became the first motorcyclist to exceed 90mph for the hour, though the following year his average was slightly down at 89.9mph. And, also using a product of the Bayerische Motoren Werke, H. W. Aldington averaged 98.52mph in his 328 BMW. Speeds were getting close to 100mph and the Club President, L. A. Baddeley, put up a trophy for the first competitor to cover 100 miles in the hour.

Best performances put up at the 1937 meeting by what were essentially tuned road vehicles show what was by then being achieved: F. E. Elgood (4,398cc Bentley), 98.00mph; F. R. Gerard (1,496cc Riley Sprite), 83.03mph; W. W. S. Bennett (1,496cc Alta), 84.3mph; A. Watson ($1^{1}/_{2}$-

1929: Little did the owners of these standard-looking production sports cars, taking part in the Brooklands One-Hour High-Speed Trial, realise the immense values they would one day command as Vintage Sports Cars.

litre Aston Martin), 81.64mph; F. A. Thatcher (1,287cc MG Magnette), 84.41mph; E. Hazledonk (939cc MG PB Midget), 84.41mph; E. W. Day (490cc Norton), 91.34mph; and D. Parkinson (250cc Excelsior), 81.64mph.

So popular and successful had the Brooklands meetings become that applications were made to the authorities for two bookings in 1938, on 25 June and 17 September. The first of these was not available, so an approach was made to Fred Craner who, as secretary of the Derby and District Motor Club, was responsible for organising events at Donington. Thus came about the MCC's first Donington Meeting With only 46 motor-cycles and 58 cars entered for the two five-lap and two 20-lap handicap events, this new road circuit could not approach the Brooklands track, though a contemporary report was headed 'New Venture Provides Exciting Racing'.

It was in 1938, at the last of the MCC's Brooklands meetings, that the magic 100 miles in the hour were first exceeded – and by more than one competitor. F. E. Elgood's Bentley, listed at 4,496cc (enlarged; it had been 4,398 the previous year), covered 110.31 miles, the greatest distance of all. He was followed by H. J. Aldington's Frazer Nash-BMW with 107.1 miles, Sir Lionel Phillips's 7,200cc Leyland with 106.71 and G. A. Wood's 3,008cc Talbot with 103.22. What is more, the 'magic ton' was also exceeded in the motor-cycle field, J. Kentish's 998cc Vincent HRD covering 100.6 miles.

Though the September 1939 meeting at Brooklands had to be cancelled, World War II having already started, the Donington meeting was held on 1 July with, as recorded in the Minutes, ' . . .entries coming in very slowly'.

Looking back at the steadily increasing speeds put up during these Brooklands meetings, especially in the flying-lap 'Dash', one can not help wondering how many miles today's 'super-bikes' and the exotic Aston Martins, Ferraris and the like – and, come to that, their humbler, mass-produced counterparts – would have covered in the hour if these meetings had continued under identical conditions on the old Brooklands track.

With Brooklands surrendered for ever to the massed onslaughts of the aircraft industry and nine years of tree growth and general decay, and with Donington still occupied in strength by the Army, the immediate post-World War II years were bleak for the MCC so far as speed events were concerned. Other clubs more race-orientated than the MCC and with fewer rival interests on their hands were managing somehow. Notable among these was the Cambridge University AC whose ambitious and far-seeing race meeting in June 1946 at Gransden Lodge, a Pathfinder Group airfield on the Huntingdonshire-Cambridgeshire borders, is now part of motor-racing history. This event proved conclusively that successful race-meetings could be run on disused airfields – and that motor-racing was once more possible in England.

Two such airfield circuits were to grow famous through the years. One was Westhampnett – satellite of Tangmere, at Goodwood – where the Goodwood Circuit was opened officially on 18 September 1948 by the Duke of Richmond and Gordon for its first race-meeting. The other was Silverstone, where the inaugural meeting was held on 2 October 1948 as the RAC British Grand Prix, run with the BRDC who had leased and developed the old wartime airfield. Petrol rationing was still strictly in force; and the Labour Government demanded an Entertainment Tax amounting to forty-six per cent of the total takings – as well as imposing very harsh restrictions on building for other than essential purposes. Such was the enthusiasm to re-create the sport that even these restrictions were unable to prevent the meetings from being outstanding successes.

The first indication of the MCC's interest in Silverstone as a possible replace-

ment for Brooklands came at the Committee meeting on 18 May 1949, when
J. C. Lowe enquired whether there were any prospects of using the circuit for
a meeting. The Secretary undertook to obtain full details from the RAC, the
outcome of which was a booking with the RAC for 9 September 1950, the
Secretary agreeing to discuss details with Col Stanley Barnes, Competitions
Manager of the RAC. At the same time – and for many years previously –
Committee member A. C. Cookson had been investigating the possibility of
the MCC establishing their own motor-racing circuit and, possibly, hill-climb
course. He reported on 17 January 1950 that he had discovered ground that
was not only available but would accommodate a circuit with a lap length
of $4^1/_2$ to 5 miles. The Club paid out £100 in solicitor's searchings and
surveyor's fees, and the estimated cost of building the circuit was to have
been £150,000. This, however, appears to have been the last mention of the
project – presumably because of the availability of Silverstone.

With the RAC's permission to use the circuit granted, a Silverstone sub-
committee was chosen, and it was at first felt that the 1950 meeting should be
a 'closed' event with one-hour and half-hour high-speed regularity trials and a

1953: The changing face of Club President, Basil de Mattos – this time taking a
'Gold' in the High-Speed Trial at Silverstone. With a twist-grip adrift, he jammed
the throttle wide-open with a matchstick for the entire hour's run.

$^1/_4$-mile timed trial – reproducing in effect the 'Blind' and the 'Dash' of pre-war Brooklands days. At the same time it was suggested that the twelve clubs using the Silverstone circuit for race meetings should form a Supporters' Club, enabling members of all twelve clubs to attend any of the twelve meetings. This received unanimous support, and Major Marians and Leslie Freeman were appointed to raise the matter at the RAC Clubs Conference on 10 March – at which arrangements were put in hand for its formation. This seemingly good idea was subsequently abandoned.

The regulations were drawn up for a series of four 45-minute high-speed reliability trials (not races), divided between motor-cycles and cars according to entries and entitled the MCC Silverstone High-Speed Trial; and eight 3-lap scratch races divided again as above. Classes for all events were laid down: Motor-cycles: 125, 250, 350, 500, and unlimited cc. Cars: 1,100, 1,500, 2,000, 2,500 and unlimited cc. Entry fees for the 45-minute events were set at £2 for cars and £1 for motor-cycles; and for the 3-lap events, 10s for motor-cycles and £1 for cars. Entries for each event were restricted to fifty motor-cycles and thirty cars, as laid down at the time with one car per $^1/_{10}$-mile of circuit on the 3-mile lap of the 1949 Silverstone, which was reduced to 2.89 miles in 1950. This ruling didn't seem to apply to high-speed trials, however; the Eight Clubs found at their meeting on 3 June that forty cars could be started 'quite conveniently' in such events. The MCC programme was amended accordingly.

During the weeks before this initial exploratory 1950 Silverstone meeting members of the sub-committee attended meetings run by other clubs, and learned a lot. And when the time came, despite bad weather, the meeting went off well with around thirty each of cars and motor-cycles. This nowhere near compared with the record entry of 240 at Brooklands in 1927, nor even the smallest pre-war of 131 in 1931, but it was a start. Takings at the car park came to £106 6s 5d and the sale of programmes brought in £40 14s – a total of £147 0s 5d (less Entertainment Tax).

As a result of experience gained at this meeting, the sub-committee made various suggestions for changes in 1951: That all vehicles should be in full touring trim and licensed for road use; that the entry fee should be adjusted to include competitors' Third Party insurance; and that the following events should be held: Three one-hour speed trials (one for motor-cycles, two for cars); one 5-lap scratch race each for cars and motor-cycles; one 5-lap handicap race each for cars and motor-cycles; and one 5-lap Winners' Handicap race each for cars and motor-cycles (with the first four finishers in each of the scratch and handicap races taking part). They also recommended the following schedule of average speeds and distances required in the One-Hour High Speed Reliability

Trials to qualify for awards:

	First Class Award		Second Class Award		Third Class Award	
	Laps	Speed mph	Laps	Speed mph	Laps	Speed mph
Motor-cycles						
125cc	16	36.48	15	34.30	14	29.64
250cc	19	43.32	18	41.40	19	38.76
350cc	22	50.16	21	47.88	20	45.60
500cc	24	54.72	23	52.44	22	50.16
Unlimited	25	57.00	24	54.72	23	52.44
350cc sidecar	18	41.04	17	38.76	16	36.48
600cc sidecar	21	47.88	20	45.60	19	43.32
Unlimited side car and three-wheelers	22	50.16	21	47.88	20	45.60
Cars						
1,100cc	21	47.88	20	45.60	19	43.32
1,500cc	22	50.16	21	47.88	20	45.60
2,000cc	23	52.44	22	50.16	21	47.88
2,500cc	24	54.72	23	52.44	22	50.16
3,000cc	25	57.00	24	54.72	23	52.44
Unlimited	26	59.28	25	57.00	24	54.72

These average speed requirements make an interesting comparison with the performances of which today's motor-cycles and cars are capable. Later in the year they were amended slightly, the upper limit for the 1,100cc car class being raised to 1,300cc, and the number of laps required for each Class Award being increased by one for car classes up to 1,300cc and up to 1,500cc, and reduced by one for three-wheelers. Both the RAC and ACU issued Closed Invitation permits and again the meeting went off successfully.

During September 1951 it seems there were misgivings about the future of Silverstone as a racing circuit, but the British Racing Drivers' Club invited the 'Silverstone clubs' to a meeting on 29 November 1951 at which all doubts were dispelled – and, for a hire charge of £50, the circuit was booked for the 1952 meeting on 13 September. This was again run under a Closed Invitation permit, the following clubs being invited: Bentley DC, Bristol MC and LCC,

1985: Although the entry is now confined to motor-cycles and three-wheelers, on the grounds of safety, the Silverstone race meetings still have much of the atmosphere of the pre-war Brooklands events.r the entire hour's run.

BARC, Vintage SCC, MG Car Club, Civil Service MA and Exmoor MC. The car classes in the High Speed Trial were again adjusted (to 1,100, 1,500, 2,500 and unlimited cc). By now the 1.608-mile Club Circuit had been created and it was agreed to fix the target speeds for different engine-capacity classes in the High Speed Trial later in the season, based on experience gained by other clubs using the new circuit. The Team Relay Race for cars was enlivened by the introduction of a compulsory 'pit stop' with some definite object, such as changing a sparking-plug. In contrast with today's strict requirements regarding safety, the RAC did not require either medical certificates or crash-helmets in the High Speed Trials for cars.

After inspecting the new Club Circuit the Silverstone sub-committee felt that Woodcote corner was dangerous, particularly with the large number of competitors likely to turn up for MCC events. A letter was written to Desmond Scannell, Secretary of the BRDC, asking if there would be any objection to setting up a chicane at Woodcote, with the required speeds in

the High Speed Trials remaining the same. Scannell replied that there would
be no objection to this.

An almost all-time record entry was received for the 1952 meeting –
even including the old Brooklands days – with a total of 197 (102 cars and
95 motor-cycles). As a result, an additional One Hour High Speed Trial for
motor-cycles and a 5-lap handicap for cars had to be added. And, because the
journal *Motor Sport* was kind enough to put up a trophy for this meeting, there
was also the 5-lap *Motor Sport* Trophy handicap race for cars. In anticipation of
a similar increase in spectators, the print order for programmes was increased
to 3,000.

Starting at 10am and finishing at 6.45pm the meeting was blessed by
perfect weather and from start to finish the lengthy programme ran to time,
closing with the *Motor Sport* 5-lap handicap. For the second year in succession
the Bentley Drivers' Club won the Relay Race. For the sidecar entries, though,
it was a disappointing day. Lack of knowledge of the new 1.608-mile Club
Circuit, let alone the effect the Woodcote chicane might have upon it – and,
more particularly, the absence of any feed-back from other clubs using this
combination of circuit-plus-chicane – resulted in a total lack of claims for
awards among the sidecar entries in their One Hour High Speed Trial. History
does not record the number of protests received by the Stewards as a result
of this, though with the sporting nature of this particular class of competitor
there may well have been none. Hurried calculations based, now, on hard-won
experience made certain this would not happen again.

Relaxed and happy though the Brooklands meetings had been, their
successors at Silverstone were beginning to overtake them, both as entry- and
crowd-pullers. And the MCC was keeping abreast of the changing face of post-
war motor and motor-cycle racing, gaining experience of conditions entirely
different from those at Brooklands and with a new generation of competitors;
and overcoming the snags – not all of them under their control or of their own
making.

By the 1953 meeting – fourth in the Silverstone series – the sporting
calendar was becoming so crowded that the traditional September date was
impossible; major meetings at Goodwood and Brands Hatch were already taking place on the only two dates available at Silverstone, and the meeting was
moved forward to 3 July. With its unpredictable effect on lap speeds for the
various motor-cycle categories, yet its desirability in reducing speeds through
the fast Woodcote corner, the chicane came up for discussion once more. Basil
de Mattos, with long experience of competing in, as well as organising such
events, recorded his 'complete disapproval of any sort of chicane whatever'.
He lost the day, though. It was retained, though eased slightly; and after

the meeting it was criticised for being 'not difficult enough'. Crash helmets became compulsory for drivers and their (also compulsory) passengers in open cars, ten helmets being hired from the ACU for 1 shilling (5p) each.

The Silverstone sub-committee for the 1954 meeting was elected in January of the year, and made a start by asking Jimmy Brown, then Track Manager for the BRDC, what alternative circuits he could make available. Whatever he may have been able to offer, it was decided to use the old Club Circuit as it simplified the programme arrangements – though not, it seems, the schedule of required speeds in the One-Hour trials, which had to be revised in the absence of the controversial chicane. Entries eventually closed at 231 – closer still to the all-time record – and were made up as follows:

One-Hour Trial: motor cycles	63	
cars	64	
5-lap scratch race: motor cycles	22	
cars	14	
5-lap handicap: motor-cycles	21	
cars	38	
Team Handicap for cars	9	(three teams)

The entry would have been considerably larger had it been possible to extend the 12 June closing date as the office was inundated by late entries, all of which had to be turned down. Matters at the office were further complicated by an accident to the long-serving and indispensable Mrs Harris in which she had fractured her left ankle, and sprained her right ankle. Ever conscious of the need for a fair assessment of target speeds in the One-Hour trials, the sub-committee were horrified to find, following the meeting, that they had pitched the motor-cycle speeds too high. An examination of the results, however, disclosed that the very poor showing in the second motor-cycle trial was due to bad weather. A high proportion of 'Firsts' had been obtained in the first, which had been dry – a case of *force majeur*. The only complaint had been the BRDC's ambulance which, it was claimed, had been in a scruffy and unserviceable condition.

Among the noteworthy car entries was Arthur Baker's 'racing' Land-Rover which regularly reached 70mph through Maggotts and lapped at 56mph, to the delight of the crowds. Later in the year, while Arthur and I were attending the Swiss GP at Berne, he put his remarkable vehicle in for some very extensive race tuning – which resulted in a performance far beyond its handling powers.

At a subsequent club meeting, this great and popular enthusiast inverted it on a corner and suffered fatal injuries.

Riding on the crest of the wave of post-World War II enthusiasm, the Silverstone meetings continued to attract strong entries during the early and middle 1950s; but as the sixties approached, the number of car entries began steadily to fall off. At the 1959 Silverstone meeting, for example, there were double the number of motor-cycle entries and events, as compared with the cars. Despite this, the meeting continued as a joint event until 1973 by which time I suspect it had served its purpose; there were various reasons for this.

When the MCC had first started running race meetings at Brooklands in the 1920s there were very few race meetings indeed in this country – whereas, with the multiplicity of disused airfield circuits after World War II, there were perhaps four or five minor race meetings every weekend throughout spring and summer. The calendar had become saturated. And, in the interests of safety in this proliferation of speed events, the RAC naturally enough introduced several safety requirements on the cars taking part. Production saloons, for example, nearly all had toughened glass windscreens, but for racing the rules specified laminated glass and competitors were faced by the cost of replacement. Racing, even at club level, was becoming much more specialised – and expensive – and few of the cars taking part in the MCC classic trials could compete in races without modification. Also, for some reason, a division was developing between cars and motor-cycles so far as race-meetings were concerned, competitors preferring to run at meetings held exclusively for their own category.

The final straw was the introduction of Armco barriers, first used at Monte Carlo to protect the Grand Prix cars from kerbstones, buildings, precipitous drops and suchlike during the round-the-houses Monaco GP. These were quickly adopted on British circuits, but whereas Armco is an excellent safeguard for cars, it is very dangerous for motor-cycles. So, for motor-cycle events, the Armco had to be protected by straw bales – which, in turn, are dangerous for cars because the wheels tend to clamber up them, capsizing the car; and, worse still, they can easily catch fire. It became virtually impossible, therefore, to run mixed meetings for cars and motor-cycles.

With the latter category forming more than fifty per cent of the entries, it was decided in 1974 to run the Silverstone meetings exclusively for motor-cycles, with the straw-bales remaining in place throughout the meetings. Latterly, the tendency has been to protect the Armco barriers with tyres, catering for both categories – but by the time of this innovation the die had been cast . . .and, after all, it is The Motor Cycling Club.

CHAPTER 10

The Forgotten Event

Alongside the four widely acclaimed MCC 'classics', one or two MCC events have been created and grown steadily in stature through the years to become classics in their own right – only to be abandoned for one reason or another in the fullness of time. By far the most noteworthy of these was the Inter-Team Trial for motor-cycles, which was first held in 1904 and, with gaps during the two World Wars, continued for sixty years until it was last held in 1964. To most clubs such longevity would be a source of considerable pride, but for the MCC it comes under the heading of 'ships that pass . . .' or as H. W. Tucker-Peake described it in the MCC journal *Triple*, 'The Forgotten Event'. It is to 'Tucker' (General Secretary at the time of writing, whose successors, male and female, have featured repeatedly in MCC affairs for many years) that I am indebted for the background to these notes on the event.

'The forgotten event' – the Team Trial cannot be described in any other way, as it has not been run since 1964. Older members don't seem to talk about it, and new members probably haven't heard of it. The first Team Trial was run in 1904, and for many years until the 1930s it was basically a non-stop event, timed from start to finish over a 50-100-mile road route, probably covered twice or more. Later it became shorter and rougher, and latterly developed into a very sporting event with non-stop, sub-divided trials sections and no time schedule.

The Motor Cycle, during the years through which the event was run, presented a total of six very handsome Challenge Trophies, and the official title became The Inter-Club Team Trial for *The Motor Cycle* Trophy. A team consisted of six riders, entered by a club – the club also having to provide at least two marshals for its team to qualify as a starter. To win the Trophy outright, a club had to win the event three times. It was won outright in 1908, 1924, 1931, 1947 and 1954. The first Trial was held on 27 May 1904, starting from Bicester; five teams competed and the Coventry Club won with 485 marks out of a possible 600.

Officially, the Trial did not take place in 1905. The Auto Cycle Club (later the ACU) put a ban on the event because the MCC had failed to apply to them – as the governing body of motor-cycle sport – for a permit. However, since the MCC was not affiliated to the ACC, such an application seemed neither necessary nor appropriate, and regulations were issued to four clubs, of which the Cardiff MCC, Coventry MCC, and the Essex and Beaumont MCC sent in their entry forms. Standing firmly to their rights, the ACC sent them letters threatening suspension if they took part in the event – and all three clubs withdrew, leaving only the MCC, who went ahead as planned. The team consisted of E. March (Phoenix Trimo), J. van Hooydonk (Phoenix Trimo), A. Candler (Quadrant), C. W. Brown (FN), Chester Fox (Trafalgar) and R. G. Booth (Ormind) – three solos and three sidecar outfits.

Rain fell heavily on the start at Watton-at-Stone, near Stevenage, and three competitors dropped out during the first 50 miles; but Brown, Booth and March (who completed the first leg non-stop) went on to make further non-stop performances, scoring 375 marks out of a possible 600 to win the trophy. But the previous year's winners, Coventry, refused to return the trophy until they had been given the opportunity to defend their title, and the MCC solicitors were instructed to apply for its immediate return and, if necessary, institute proceedings for its recovery. Further details of this potentially interesting fracas are unfortunately not recorded.

A contemporary issue of *The Gazette* (the MCC's monthly publication) records the reactions of the Press, of whom the club said that they '. . .were not acting with fairness in this matter'. It was stated in the Press '. . .that they (the MCC) did not acknowledge a ruling body . . .that they did not wish to rule themselves, and did not want anybody else to rule . . .' *The Gazette* commented ' . . .a more misleading statement of the attitude of the MCC could hardly have been put into so few words'.

By 1906 the differences between the club and the ACC had somehow been settled and a proposal was made at the AGM in January 1907 to apply for affiliation at a fee of 2s (10p) per motor-cycle member. The course was the same for the 1906 and 1907 events, five clubs entering for each with the MCC and the Coventry Club respectively taking the prize.

A more demanding, hillier course near Banbury was used for the 1908 event and, out of nine entries, Coventry won for the third time and thus kept the cup. *The Motor Cycle* stepped in with a second, fifty guinea Trophy, and a change in the regulations required only a single passenger machine per team (instead of two) and – so far as can be ascertained – the 1908 course was again used in 1909 and 1910, the MCC winning in 1909 as the only team to complete the 100-mile route without an involuntary stop. The following year both the Coventry and Northampton clubs finished complete, but as Coventry recorded the smallest error they became the winners yet again. For the 1911 event, the old 1904 course was resumed and three clubs completed it without a stop – the Derby and District, North West London, and South East London MCCs. Derby won with a total error of 66min 32sec, followed by North West London with 79min 8sec.

No fewer than twenty-five teams took part in 1912 over a hilly course near Daventry, five teams completing the event without incurring penalty marks – the Nottingham, Bedford, South Birmingham, Bristol, and Walthamstow MCCs, Nottingham beating Bedford by 7min 15sec to win the event. For

They also work for their sport; club members repairing Bamford Clough after the ravages of time had made this traditional MCC hill a shade too competitive

the 1913 and 1914 events a new course at Chipping Norton was used, with a record entry of forty-one (246 riders) and thirty-two respectively. Sheffield and Hallamshire MCC, and the MCC itself, were the two winners.

After a break for World War I, the Trial was resumed in 1919, and for the next nine years a course in the Chilterns was used. Up to and including 1923 it was based at Tring and, for the first time, a consistency riding test was introduced on Aston Hill. For 1924 Aston Rowant became the headquarters, and the consistency test was carried out on Alms Hill. The following year the start was from Kingston Blount, both Alms Hill and some of the 'green' roads were retained. Winning teams in the first seven post-war trials were as follows: 1919, Coventry and Warwickshire (15 entries); 1920, Leicester and District (28); 1921, Sheffield and Hallamshire (28); 1922, Woolwich, Plumstead and District (27); 1923, Nottingham (25); 1924, Coventry and Warwickshire – winning the Trophy outright for the second time (22); and 1923, Coventry and Warwickshire (20).

Once again the course was changed, moving into the Chilterns for 1926 with the start at High Wycombe, cutting out the green roads but retaining Alms Hill. Two of the eighteen teams finished complete, with the Sutton Coldfield and North Birmingham Auto Club scoring the more consistent figures. The Ilkley and District club won the 1927 event, over the same course, out of thirty team entries. In search of tougher terrain, the course for 1928 was moved northwards to the Buxton area; of the thirteen entrants, Ilkley again won the cup, with a combined error of only thirteen seconds. Theoretically the 1929 event should have been run over the old 1926 course, but 'interference with the route-markers' caused chaos on the third circuit; the results were decided on the scores established during the first two circuits, Enfield being declared the winners.

The programme for the 1930 event lists van Hooydonk, J. W. G. Brooker and Geoffrey Smith as stewards; L. A. Baddeley as clerk of the course; and T. F. Bidlake as timekeeper and secretary of the event – names that had been associated with MCC events for many years past, and were to continue so for many years to come. The start was again from Daws Hill, High Wycombe, and the MCC won in a field of twenty-one teams. Representing the club were: Len Heath (497cc Ariel sidecar), J. J. Boyd-Harvey (400cc Matchless), J. R. Watkins (346cc LGC), A. S. Denyer (500cc Douglas), George Brough (986cc Brough Superior), and V. L. Freeman (495cc Matchless) with Mrs Marjorie Freeman – his usual 'bouncer' – in the chair. This appears to have been the last trial in which Leslie Freeman competed, having been a member of the MCC team since 1924 and representing the London MCC for many years before that. The Ilkley team was second, all six of their riders on 596cc

1982: Veteran sidecar rider Jack Pouncey, who started riding in MCC events in the late twenties (and who still turns out regularly as an official) is seen here in difficulties on Lymer Rake, during the London-Edinburgh Trial.

Scott machines – a fine display of patriotism since the factory producing these memorable water-cooled twin-cylinder two-strokes was at Shipley, in Yorkshire. Another notable team in the 1930 event was that of the Birmingham MCC: D. K. Mansell (Norton sidecar), H. S. Perry (Ariel sidecar), G. B. Goodman (Norton), A. E. Perrigo (BSA), Vic Brittain (Norton) and F. E. Thacker (Ariel). Older readers will spot some of these as household names in the world of motor-cycle trials during the thirties.

Always entirely distinct from the three long-distance trials, run by the MCC for 'everyday' riders/drivers with 'ordinary' vehicles, the Inter-Club Team Trial catered for out-and-out trials riders with their specialised machines which, for example, did not require lights or, in later years, generators either and were fitted with large-section knobbly rear tyres, high-level exhaust systems and so on. As purpose-built, or converted machines developed, it was inevitable that the courses themselves became progressively tougher, and from 1930 onwards they took on an increasingly sporting nature.

Writing of the early events in the series, Leslie Freeman said:

In the twenties it was quite a test of stamina to cover 100 miles non-stop

1951: Only part of Bill Boddy was accommodated in the 1921 JAP-engined Tamplin cyclecar in which he accompanied owner Neil Smith on the *Exeter* – only to retire after being towed up Fingle Bridge, a gallant effort.

on a 33-mile course, starting, say, from Tring, up the hill to Wiggington waterworks, and on to Whyte Leaf, Kop and Alms hills . . .Some of the ingenious improvisations employed to top-up petrol tanks while still on the move had to be seen to be believed – although, strangely enough, I do not remember a single case of anyone setting himself on fire. . . .Those were the days of 28 by 3in, hard tyres, and stiff leather Brookes saddles.

For 1931 the old concept prevailed, with the course still in the Chilterns, starting from High Wycombe. Ilkley won again, making it their third victory as a result of which they won the cup outright.

Now with the fourth new cup to be presented by *The Motor Cycle*, it was for the 1932 event that major changes in the rules were introduced. The non-stop, start-to-finish requirement was abandoned, to be replaced by a series of stiff, non-stop sections; and a new system of marking was introduced whereby competitors scored points based on the distance they had climbed up each of the sections. Out of 26 team entries, the Carshalton MCC won by one second on a tie-decider from the West Middlesex MCC. Awards were now given to all competitors who finished without loss of marks, and 87 individual riders, out of a total of 156, qualified for these souvenir awards.

For 1933 and 1934 the event again broke new ground, with the start in the Stroud area – actually from the foot of the first observed section, Sandy Lane – and it was in this event that the names of well known 'trials hills' began to appear: Sandy Lane itself, Bismore, Ferriscourt, Knapp, Nailsworth Ladder, and Catswood. The Ilkley and Birmingham MCCs were the respective winners. For some reason or other – perhaps because there was no need to tax machines running on private ground – the 1935 and 1936 events were held on War Department land, respectively in the Farnham and Camberley areas. Sixteen teams competed in 1935, the Sunbeam MCC winning the cup, followed by Birmingham second, and Coventry third; at Camberley it was only ten teams, with the Sunbeam MCC again the winners, followed by Carshalton, and Witley.

For the next ten years, during which World War II came and went, the event was shelved, reappearing in 1946, again on War Department land (or Ministry of Defence, as it is now) in the Fleet area; twenty-four teams entered, with the Aldershot MCC appropriately the winners. It remained on War Department land in 1947, with a short scramble course near Liphook. The Sunbeam MCC won for their third time, and the ever-generous *Motor Cycle* produced their fifth fifty-guinea Trophy.

For some reason, perhaps because of yet another new cup, *The Motor Cycle* and the MCC agreed to abandon the sporting courses and revert to the Trial's original status as a true road event in 1948. A twenty-five mile circuit in the Stroud area was covered twice; twenty-four teams took part, with the Nottingham Tornado MCC the winners. Virtually the same course was used in 1949 and 1950, with the Weyburn MCC winning both events; and in 1951 the Trial returned to the Buxton area, where the Bradford MCC won.

Little consideration had been given so far to the Westcountry clubs, who – when they had entered, which was not often – had had to travel long distances to the starting points. A course at Dunster was chosen for 1952, apparently of very little benefit to the clubs in the south-west, for the Solihull MCC won. Back went this nomadic event to the Stroud area for 1953, where the Bradford MCC won – and to Harrogate for 1954, where Bradford won again. Since this was their third win, the cup became theirs, and *The Motor Cycle* once again put their hands in their pockets and produced their sixth – and as it turned out, their final – cup. Having apparently run short of ideas, the committee settled once and for all on the Stroud area for 1955, where the Trial was held until its demise in 1964, with a few variations. H. P. Baughan of Stroud, who was well known at the time for his attempts to transmit power to the sidecar wheel on motor-cycle sidecar outfits, was the guiding light until 1957. The routes included observed sections in the Water Lane, More Folly, Ham Hill, The BBs, Hodgscombe and Weighbridge areas, all popular trials hills at the time. Winners in 1955, 1956 and 1957 were the Leicester, Stratford-upon-Avon and West of England MCCs.

Apathy seems now to have taken over; there was no Trial in 1958 for the very good reason that nobody could be found to organise it. The ever-helpful H. W. Tucker-Peake – 'Tucker', who had been representing the MCC in these events on, among other machines, one of his Vincent-HRD Pythons – landed the contract without a lot of difficulty for 1959, becoming organiser and clerk of the course. A moderately sporting circuit was used, starting

1955: Gathering of the clans – four families well known through the years in the organisation of MCC events enjoy themselves during a route-reconnaissance for the Derbyshire Trial – the Davises, Wilsons, Freemans, and Tucker-Peakes.

from the Peusdown Inn on the A40 between Northleach and Cheltenham; once again the 'home team, the Cheltenham MCC won out of 22 teams (still made up of six riders per team). Sticking to the Drapers Farm area, the 1960 event started from The Air Balloon Inn on the lofty heights of Cleeve Hill above Cheltenham, covering two laps of a twenty-five mile, sporting circuit, and providing the Windlesham MCC with a win.

By now the writing was clearly on the wall. For 1961 Gerry Woolcott (results secretary at the time of writing) took over the organisation. Only 19 teams entered, and this figure was achieved only by reducing the number of riders per team to three. Witley and District MCC won with a loss of nineteen marks – twelve marks better than Windlesham who were second. Sadly, the last event was run in 1964, with A. C. Wyatt clerk of the course and Woolcott secretary of the meeting. Even the MCC themselves failed to enter a team. There were twelve entries, and the Bristol MCC beat the opposition by a slender five points.

Following a committee meeting on 17 December 1964, Minute 172 reads: 'Inter-Club Team Trial: After considerable discussion, taking note of the falling entries, the difficulty in finding a suitable course, and the possibility that the event in its present form has outlived its usefulness, it was proposed and seconded that the Inter-Club Team Trial would not be run in 1965.'

The donors of the Trophy had always wished that the event could have a road route, and that it would be suitable for ordinary road machines, like the Exeter, Edinburgh and Land's End trials. The event had strayed far from these ideals since the 1950s; and, especially in view of the impending Government control of road events, it was unlikely ever to return to them. So, with many problems to be faced, and much indecision as to how to solve them, this famous – and, in fact, oldest-established motor-cycle team event in the world at the time – quietly faded away.

Early in this chapter brief mention was made of an altercation between the Motor Cycling Club and the Auto Cycle Club over the running of the 1905 Inter-Team Trial. As the result of this, because the MCC had not been affiliated to the ACC and had not therefore considered it necessary to apply to them for a permit, the three clubs who had entered teams were banned by the ACC from taking part. This slight antagonism between the two bodies has surfaced from time to time, and it is interesting to look into its background – especially since *The Motor Cycle* regarded the original, 1905, confrontation as significant enough to revive it in their issue of 31 December 1977 under the heading 'MCC tactics bring sour grapes jibe'.

The Automobile Club of Great Britain and Ireland (later becoming the Royal Automobile Club in 1907 when King Edward VII gave it his patronage) was founded in 1897 by F. R. Simms, Harrington Moore and Claude Johnson (the first secretary) to provide motorists – as distinct from motor-cyclists – with a headquarters where they could discuss the new machines, attend lectures and so on. Premises were set up in a suite of rooms at 4, Whitehall Court, London at an annual rent of £400, paid for by Simms himself.

In 1903, in long-overdue recognition of the increasingly popular motor-cycle movement, the Automobile Club of Great Britain and Ireland created as an offshoot the Auto Cycle Club which was, in effect, their motor-cycle committee; F. Straight was appointed Secretary. These two organisations – the AC of GB, and the ACC – ran regular events and gatherings in their appropriate fields (such as the famous 1,000-mile trials for both categories) and became by adoption the 'governing bodies' of automobile and motor-cycle sport in the UK. In order to exert some sort of control over the increasing numbers of events, to avoid the too frequent use of popular routes, and to maintain the good name of the sport as it developed, it was natural enough that both bodies should require individual organisers to let them know what they were planning; hence the 'permits' – or go-aheads to the proposals submitted to them.

The MCC-versus-ACC differences of opinion in 1905 over the need for affiliation were not sorted out until the AGM on 14 January 1907 when a motion on behalf of the Executive was moved by the Secretary 'That in the opinion of Members the MCC apply for membership of the ACC'. This was carried; application was made officially on 11 March 1907 – and then, it seems, only on the MCC's own terms of 2s (10p) per member. Whether or not some sort of provisional affiliation had been granted in 1906 is not known, but the 1906 Inter-Team Trial had gone ahead without further argument.

The MCC was not alone in its attitude towards the governing body. In July 1907 the Newcastle MCC invited the MCC and other clubs to a meeting in Durham to discuss the whole question of affiliation and, in particular, the ACC's 'excessive fees'. However, as the ACC were holding a meeting of their Council in Lincoln, the MCC suggested that the Durham meeting be transferred to Lincoln, and held during the forenoon of the day of the ACC's Council meeting. It was agreed to reconsider the whole structure of the ACC, and it was placed on the Agenda 'That the Auto Cycle Club be reconstructed and in future be known as the Auto Cycle Union composed of affiliated clubs only, the same to control the sport of motor-cycling, and be formed by the Royal Automobile Club and a four per cent representation from all affiliated clubs in the Kingdom'. At this memorable ACC meeting, the MCC were represented by Messrs Head, Wells and van Hooydonk; and the Auto Cycle Club became known as the Auto Cycle Union – the title which this highly respected body retains today.

As a result, there lingers a tenuous though understandable claim among the older members of the MCC for paternity of the ACU. For the initials 'ACU', in part, perhaps; but it must be conceded that, just as the RAC was originally founded under a different name in 1897, so was the ACU in 1903 – and not 1907! It was, however, a little unkind and unjustified of *The Motor Cycle* to publish in 1905, and to revive in 1977: 'They don't acknowledge a ruling body, they don't want to rule themselves, and they don't want anybody else to rule.'

CHAPTER 11

The Also-rans

During the 1930s the Committee's energy seems to have been inexhaustible and more and more events were taken on. Someone spotted a gap in the calendar during the balmy month(s) of high-summer, and the London-Scarborough Trial was slotted-in on 30 July 1932, with an entry of 136 (28 solo motor-cycles, 9 three-wheelers, 4 sidecars and 95 cars). Four observed hills were included in the route (White Horse, Boltby Bank, Little Blakey and Little Beck) with a time check at Scarborough and two 200-yard tests. It can not have been a very taxing event as 16 solos, 7 sidecars, all 9 three-wheelers and 67 cars won Premier Awards. Among them were Charlie Roger (348cc Ariel), Len Gibbs (346cc Royal Enfield), George Brough and F. W. Stevenson (Brough Superiors), Reggie Tongue (Riley 9), K. N. Hutchinson (Alvis), A. B. Langley in a large $2^1/_2$-litre MG saloon, and A. L. S. Denyer (father of today's Lea Francis campaigner) on a 596cc Douglas.

So delighted were the Scarborough authorities with the event that they planned to make it a very special occasion in 1933. To cater for all tastes, and to encourage a greater entry, it was run as the Scarborough Rally and Trial on 8 June with starting points at London, Chester, Bristol, Edinburgh and Birmingham and separate routes for the trial and rally from the converging point at Harrogate to the finish at Scarborough. Instead of the anticipated 150 there were only 84 entries, and for several reasons the event was not a success. For 1934 the Committee looked at other possible areas and approaches were made to the authorities at Rhyl, Llandudno, Morecambe and Southport – resulting in a warm invitation from the Town Clerk at Llandudno. Thus came about the

1954: Waiting for their turn to start on the 50th Anniversary *Edinburgh* are George Brough on one of his own machines, Oliver Langdon on a 1903 Rex, and 'Oily' Karslake on what was then the latest (and by far the quietest) word in motor-cycles, the LE Velocette.

Llandudno Trial (alias the Welsh Trial) on 6–7 July 1934.

There were three starting points: London (Bull Hotel, Gerards Cross), Buxton (Palace Hotel) and Exeter (Bedford Garage), all three routes converg-ing on Shrewsbury for breakfast at the Raven Hotel after a run of 180 miles. The entry was much more satisfactory with 24 motor-cycles and 136 cars, and B. G. K. Rushbrook, on a 680cc Brough Superior headed the column from the breakfast halt at 6am on 7 July. The trials route that followed included observed sections on Dolywern, Allt-y-Bady, Old Bwlch, Maes-y-Safn and Bodfari hills, with the leader arriving at Llandudno at 11am for the final tests on Conway Road.

Now known loosely as the 'July Trial' because of its nomadic nature, the 1935 event was forced to abandon Llandudno because of the unfriendly 'police activities' during the RAC Rally. It was now the Town Clerk of Torquay who promised to provide a warm welcome to competitors at the finish on 27 July – not only that, but he agreed to set aside Meadfoot Sea Road and Ilsham Road for the special tests at the finish, suggesting that the Palace Hotel, being adjacent to both, might be the headquarters. The event started on Friday evening, 26 July, from London, Birmingham and Bournemouth, the three routes converging at

Deller's Cafe, Exeter, for breakfast. The subsequent trials route to the Torquay finish included observed climbs of Windout, Pepperdon, Little John, Simms and Slippery Sam; an alternative rally-type route of 50 miles was plotted for those who did not wish to climb the trials hills – though this event was known as the July Trial. This time the entry was 136, though it included only six motor-cycles.

Seeking perhaps to cater for all tastes, it became openly the Torquay Rally and Trial in 1936, with starting points at Virginia Water, Stratford-on-Avon, Penzance and Cardiff (included because another event was due to finish there on 16 July, the day before the Torquay started, and it was felt that a few enthusiasts might wish to compete in both events!). The Committee ruled that pillion passengers would be allowed on solo motor-cycles throughout the rally route, though not on those motor-cycles competing in the trial; and not on either during the special tests. The 'trials' route ran over Dartmoor, climbing the previous year's hills – except for Slippery Sam because of the number of local trials using this hill. The 140 starters (including 35 in the motor-cycle classes) faced bad weather throughout the event, and R. T. Newbury (500cc Triumph) was the only motor-cyclist to win a Premier Award; only three (R. C. Rivas, R. W. Prail and F. W. Stevenson) won Silver Medals. Of the 105 cars, 28 won PAs, one of whom was J. D. Barnes in the same $1\frac{1}{2}$-litre Singer that his son drives in today's MCC trials. Only two of the car teams finished 'clean': the Ford V8s of Darton, Thompson and Viscount Chetwynd, and the 1,408cc supercharged 'Musketeer' MGs (MacDermid, Bastock and Langley) whose aggregate time in the tests was 35 seconds quicker than that of the Fords.

By 1937 the unfortunate scribe who typed the Minutes had given up trying to keep pace with the ever-changing title, resorting in despair to 'The Torquay Event'. But the main Committee sorted things out by adopting the organising sub-committee's recommendation '. . .that the most important point is that it should be run entirely on rally lines, with no trials route'. The event held on 23–24 July, therefore, was the Torquay Rally. It was the wrong decision apparently, for only eighty-two entries were received, including all classes, with sixteen claiming Premier Awards. The trial element was reinstated for the 1938 event which became the Torquay Trial – just about the only title that had not previously been used. A new system of marking was introduced whereby competitors were credited with 500 marks at the start, deductions being made for early or late arrival at controls, failure on observed sections and failure to carry out the final tests correctly. Only Simms was an exception, with fifteen credit marks for a clean climb but no penalties for a failure. Entries fell to sixty-seven, including ten in the motor-cycle classes.

Even with the resourceful and vastly experienced Jackie Masters on the organising committee from its first conception as the London-Scarborough Trial, this event never really caught on, possibly because it was at the wrong season of the year. It was not held in 1939 but had it not been for the intervention of World War II, a Harrogate Rally might well have replaced the 'Torquay Event'. In July 1939 a letter was received from the Harrogate Corporation inviting the Club to run such an event in June 1940, an invitation that was optimistically accepted – but subsequently declined.

In 1948, still under petrol-rationing, it was decided to revive a very old title, the Devon Trial, with the start in Parlhouse Road, Minehead and the finish, thirty-four miles later, in the Station Yard, Lynmouth. The event was held on 31 July, organised by Jackie Masters and Cyril Kemp, and included observed sections on Doverhay, Yealscombe, Wellshead, Southern Wood, Lyn, Beggars' Roost and Station Lane. The entry list was strong, bearing in mind the fuel shortage, with thirty-three motor-cycles and sixty-seven cars, and it read like

For several years, the Scoot to Scotland was sponsored by Esso and run in conjunction with the London-Edinburgh, with an entry confined to the popular scooters of the day, along with 'bubble-cars' such as the Vespa and Messerschmitt.

a Who's Who of trials riders and drivers. Jimmy Green, Mrs Anning, William Bray, E. J. Bores, 'Darcy' Sugden, Arnold White, J. W. Smith and R. W. Prail were among the riders, and the drivers included Onslow-Bartlett (Mercury Special), Cyril Crossby (supercharged Vauxhall), Ken Wharton (Wharton), A. F. Scroggs (Trojan), Alf Morrish (MG), F. Morrish (Frazer Nash), Jack Radbourne, W. G. Uglow and Denis Scobey (HRGs), Peter Morgan, W. A. G. Goodall and Basil de Mattos (Morgan 4/4s), Leslie Potter, J. H. Appleton and Ken Burgess (Allards) and many more.

Best performances respectively in the motor-cycle and car classes were put up by Arnold White (Matchless) and Jack Radbourne (HRG), both Penzance men. Only nine motor-cycles and fourteen cars won Premier Awards, Yealscombe alone accounting for fifty-two failures. It was intended to run this event again in 1949 as the Minehead Trial, but difficulties arose with one or two of the observed sections, and it was abandoned. Scobey's HRG, one in a long line of exciting cars driven in MCC trials by this great enthusiast, was sold to John Aley, today's MCC Chairman, who carried on the good work.

In 1953 this odd-man-out was revived, and moved to autumn and the Cotswolds where the Autumn Trial was held on 10 October, starting at Moreton-in-the-Marsh and covering a route that included nine observed sections. The event was run in perfect weather, with the hills in easy condition; of the 124 starters, 29 solos, 3 sidecars, one three-wheeler and 19 cars claimed Premier Awards. With a strong rally flavour, the event was repeated in 1954. The start was at the Evenlode Hotel on the A40 at Eynsham with a 140-mile route that included nine special tests laid out on hard surfaces.

First held in 1921, the 'MCC Sporting' must have been a welcome newcomer for those who were beginning to wonder whether they actually belonged to a motor-cycling club, so strong was the car membership growing. The event was exclusively for solo motor-cycles and included sections far too tough for cars of the day. With starting points at either Caterham or Ripley until the 1925 event, when a move was made to the Camberley area, a twenty-mile route over Bagshot Heath was laid out, to be completed twice as a continuous run. There was no requirement for the event to be completed non-stop; but if, because of a stop, or to prevent a stop, a competitor received outside assistance, a penalty of 6min 36sec was added to the standard lap time. They wandered about the Heath from Turf Hill, on the King's Ride, via such well-known landmarks as Kilimanjaro Hill, Red Roads, Water Tower Hill, Devil's Drop, Broadmore and Twin Rise Hill.

Major changes were made for the 1929 event, ninth in the series, when sidecar outfits and cars were admitted. The start, at midnight on 26 October, was moved to Virginia Water and ran through the night to a control and the breakfast stop

1962: Much club motor sport in the late sixties and early seventies was dominated by the road-going special. The Stevenage-based team of Derek Fleming (Primrose), H. W. Tucker-Peake (Tucker-MG), Ron Warren (Dellow) and John Tucker-Peake (Minor-based, Consul-engined Olympic) take lunch on their way home from an *Exeter*.

at Askers Road House in Dorset. After a 7am re-start, competitors were faced by two laps of a route that included Meerhay, Woodhayes, Devenish Pit and Beacon – names already familiar to competitors in the *Exeter*. There were 120 entries of which 105 were classified as finishers, 30 of them winning Premier Awards.

A move was made to the Buxton area for the 1930 event, proving to be so popular that the Buxton weekend was retained throughout the life of this trial. The route turned out to be so formidable that, out of an entry of 100, H. J. Aldington's Frazer Nash was the only car to win a Premier. Three solo motor-cycles, R. B. Clark (498cc Gillet), A. L. S. Denyer (596cc Douglas) and Len Heath (497cc Ariel) won Premiers, along with two sidecar outfits – H. P. Rose (497cc Ariel) and F. H. Wallis (496cc Raleigh). Other well-known names in the entry list included: J. A. Leyland (P&M), R. F. Tingle (Scott), F. W. Stevenson (Brough), W. F. Gowlett (493cc BSA), Brooklands exponent R. T. Horton (1,096cc Morgan three-wheeler), Donald Healey (1,021cc BSA three-wheeler), F. P. Barker (Austin Seven – and still competing in MCC events), F. J. Brymer (Riley – and well-known photographer), and A. F. Scroggs in his Trojan. Among the eight observed sections were Cowdale, Pillwell Lane, Putwell and Litton Slack, the last-mentioned being omitted on the second lap of the course as it had stopped all but the six who were eventually to win Premier Awards.

In pre-World War II years entries had ranged either side of the one hundred mark, with a peak of 149 in 1935 and a steady increase in the proportion of car entries. The final pre-war 'Sporting' was held in 1938, with 113 entries; and in 1948, when it re-started, there were seventy-six of which every car and all but one solo failed Litton Slack. In 1947, out of ninety-five entries, one solo and forty cars won Premiers; and John Tucker-Peake failed on only Jenkins Chapel and Bamford Clough – riding a 1,000cc Vincent, the largest and almost certainly the most unsuitable motor-cycle ever ridden in the Buxton Sporting Trial.

By mutual agreement in 1947 the MCC and Sheffield and Hallamshire MC decided in future to run the 'Sporting' and the latter's famous High Peak Trial during the Saturday and Sunday of the same weekend, giving competitors the opportunity of running in two big trials in succession. The 'Sporting' was run under a 'Restricted Invitation' permit at the time, with the Lancashire AC, Lancs and Cheshire AC, MG Car Club, N.W. London MC, Sheffield and Hallamshire MC, West of England MC and Yorkshire Sports CC all being invited to compete.

Various changes were made to the route, strange-sounding, agricultural local names for obscure farm-tracks appearing on the route-cards, some quickly to return to the limbo they had enjoyed, others to reappear regularly through the years. By 1949 Washgates, Dow Low, Checks, Tilsbury, Jenkins Chapel, Litton Slack and Taddington were among the sections. Bamford Clough had been used since 1934; and Cow Low, Dun Cow's Grove and Old Joe's appeared for the first time in 1951. But for them their new-found publicity was short-lived, for 1951 was the last year of the 'Sporting'.

Like the 'July Trial/Rally', with its various titles, routes and characters, the Sporting Trial was not yet forgotten, reappearing in 1954 as the Derbyshire Trial. Retaining the character of the 'Sporting', this was also a tough, one-day event that made no claims to being suitable for everyday vehicles as with the three classics – though many of the competing vehicles seemed standard enough. The trial lasted for six years, using varying numbers of starting points from four in 1954 to one in 1959 (the Rootes Group's factory at Ryton-on-Dunsmore). The finish was usually either at the Palace or Rutland Arms Hotel at Bakewell where an informal dinner, film show and social evening were laid on at the end of the day.

Hills included many names familiar to the old Sporting Trial – Clough Wood, Pilsey, Putwell, Taddington, Lymer Rake, Moorside, Old Joe's, High-cliffe, Priestcliffe and Litton Slack – which, if none of the others did their bit, continued to ensure that the Club hadn't to be too lavish in the distribution of Premier Awards. In 1960 the Derbyshire Trial ceased to exist as an individual event and for various reasons was merged with the *Edinburgh*.

CHAPTER 12

MCC Personalities

More than most clubs, the MCC has always generated a strong family loyalty among its members. There are those who join to compete in certain events and allow their memberships to lapse. Others have joined, enjoyed their fill of competitions, and then – drawn by the friendships formed, and the pleasant places to which the events take them – turned to running these events (and even the Club itself), putting back into the kitty some of the pleasure they have drawn from it. The outstanding among these are recorded in the following pages; others have appeared regularly throughout the text. It is to H. W. Tucker-Peake that I am indebted for the following notes on some of the MCC's many personalities.

From the early beginnings prominent names have appeared in the entry lists: S. F. Edge, Charles Jarrott, A. G. Reynold, C. A. Vandervell, Malcolm (later Sir Malcolm) Campbell, W. O. Bentley, Victor Riley, Lionel Martin, H. F. S. Morgan, A. Frazer Nash, Lionel Baddeley, George Brough and W. R. Morris (later Lord Nuffield).

Among the motor-cycle 'regulars', competing in the long-distance events in more recent times, there have been: T. G. Meeten, Basil de Mattos, F. W. Stevenson, E. Travers, G. K. Rae, A. E. Perrigo, G. North, Henry Laird, Bill Clarke, Phil Vincent and Stan Wooldridge.

Car competitors came from a much wider field, and the *Land's End* in particular appealed to many national and even international 'names': S. C. H. Davis, Mort Morris Goodall, Oliver Bertram, Kaye Don, A. Powys-

1987: The MCC, as one of the earliest users of the track, was well represented at the opening of the Brooklands Museum. President Basil de Mattos found his Grindlay Peerless-JAP on show – raced by him half a century earlier.

Lybbe, Philip Fotheringham-Parker, Richard Seaman, George Abecassis, Peter Whitehead, Marcel Becquart, F. A. Thatcher, Geoffrey Taylor, D. G. and K. D. Evans, H. W. Inderwick, W. M. Couper, R. J. W. Appleton, and J. A. Daiskell who drove (among other cars) his French-built Rally before running it in the Brooklands Double-Twelve race.

The well-known 'names' in the one-day sporting trials of the 1930s, too, were prominent: 'Grasshopper' Austin Sevens (Buckley, Langley and Scriven); Batten Ford V8s (Batten, Inderwick and Murray-West); 'Jabberwock' Ford V8s (Norton, Loader and Koppenhagen); Ford V8 coupes (Denton, Clelland and Viscount Chetwynd); HRGs (Robins, Curtis and Undery); 'Cream Cracker' MGs (Toulmin, Crawford and Jones); 'Musketeer' MGs (Macdermid, Bastock and Langley); Morgan (H. F. S and P. H. G. Morgan and W. A. Goodall); 1½-litre Singers (Langley, Barnes and Billingham).

Last, but by no means least, there is Harvey Postlethwaite, designer in the Grand Prix field of the Hesketh and, until recently, Ferraris, who drove a Morgan in a team with Geoff Margetts, today's Treasurer and Membership Secretary. The MCC, it seems, is all things to all men!

F. T. BIDLAKE

For ever remembered as Trials Secretary, Official Timekeeper, and the moving force behind many, many *Land's End*, *Exeter* and *Edinburgh* trials, 'Biddy' was already well known as a racing cyclist – and prize-winner in the North Road 24 Hours event of 1888 – long before he became involved with the MCC. He was President of the North Road Club from 1914 to 1933, and President of the Roads Records Association from 1924 to 1933 – more often seen, apparently, on a tricycle than a bicycle. He held the 100 miles record on a push-bike in 1891, with a time of 6 hours 16 minutes 27 seconds.

Having abandoned the energetic sport of cycling as the years advanced, he became Official Timekeeper for the MCC, ACU, RAC and RAeC – thus having the distinction of timing the Schneider Trophy air races. He devised complicated electrical apparatus for timing stop-and-re-start tests, and even produced a bulky and complicated electrical device for measuring a run-back-over-line fault.

Ironically, he died on 17 September 1933 following an accident while riding a push-bike down Barnet Hill in August. A sizeable fund of over £1,000 was collected, and was used for a memorial to 'Biddy', set up at Popular Corner, Girtford Bridge, near Sandy (on the Great North Road). The centre-piece, a sundial, is inscribed 'He Measured Time'.

ARTHUR BONWICK

An enthusiastic worker, 'Bonnie' joined the Committee in 1961, and from then onwards was either Secretary or Clerk of the Course – sometimes both – at the Silverstone meetings from 1962 until 1984; and he took on the demanding jobs of Membership Secretary and Executive Chairman from 1980.

During World War II he served in the Army in both France and Burma. Before the Dunkirk evacuation he was stranded some 200 miles behind the German lines in France, and covered this distance on foot, mostly at night, escaping capture and reaching Dunkirk in time to be ferried to England.

A devoted motor-cyclist throughout his life, Bonnie died peacefully in his sleep at Sidmouth – on the night when many Club members were journeying to Sidmouth during the 1985 Exeter Trial.

Arthur Bonwick, Chairman, Membership Secretary and Organiser of the Silver-stone meetings, who died in 1985 whilst on the Exeter Trial, was respected by all. Despising the comfort of four wheels, he was a staunch motor-cyclist.

W. ('BILL') CALDWELL

An extremely active competition member, driving various Rileys and Triumph TRs from the TR2 to the TR5, Bill was a professional BEA pilot – and possessed, apparently, of unlimited energy. On many occasions he would return from a long flight to Heathrow, collect his car from the car park and drive straight to the start of a trial. He became a regular Travelling Marshal, and when he blurted out a 'request' in his broad Scots accent, you took it as an order.

On retirement from BEA, he moved to New Zealand where he was employed flying Walrus machines – his old wartime job. He died in December 1984 as the result of a stroke.

S. C. H. ('SAMMY') DAVIS

Racing motorist, Le Mans winner, trials driver, motoring journalist, artist and Sports Editor of *The Autocar* from pre-World War I until 1950, Sammy found time also to be an enthusiastic competitor in MCC events for many years. Together with Arthur Bourne – editorial director of *The Autocar* and *The Motor Cycle*, and MCC Committee member and trials official for most of the inter-wars years – Sammy was a firm believer in the value of motor-cycles as a training ground for car driving, and he started his MCC career before World War I on a Motosacoche with 'light pedal assistance'.

In one of his charmingly written memoirs he describes riding this grossly underpowered 'moped' in a pre-World War I *Edinburgh*, during which he pedalled the entire route from London to York before the engine could be persuaded to develop enough power to take over – even then, only intermittently. By the time he was forced to abandon trials driving in 1933, due mainly to the increasing pressures of motor racing and his journalistic career, he had driven well over a dozen different makes of car in MCC events – including ABC, AC, front-wheel-drive Alvis (in which he finished eighth at Le Mans in 1928), Frazer Nash, MG, Lagonda – and an extremely low-built Brooklands Riley which (intended by its creators for speed events on smooth racing circuits) must have been one of the least suitable cars ever to run in the *Land's End* at the time.

V. L. FREEMAN

Leslie first joined the MCC in 1921 and has been an active member almost ever since, serving on the Committee from 1924 until 1974 – including the posts of Treasurer, Chairman and President.

His first trial was the *Edinburgh* in 1921 – the last occasion on which the trial started from the Gatehouse at Highgate, before moving to the Police

College at Hendon in 1922. Writing in the first issue of the Club's magazine *Triple*, Leslie reckoned that if a non-stop section had been included at the top of Page Street, Mill Hill, many awards would have been lost – a considerable proportion of the entry having come to rest on the steep left-turn into Wise Street, such were the shortcomings of those early motor-cycles.

Leslie's mount in 1921 was a heavy 8hp Sunbeam with a large Milford sidecar in which his father travelled in comparative luxury. They were included in the Matchless works team, along with Tommy Ross and Wilf Gulver, who predicted they would not finish. They did, however – but very late. Turning out regularly in the three classic trials during the following nine years, Leslie won several Premier Awards – with three Triple Awards to his, and his wife Marjorie's, credit.

Their daughter Daphne, too, was a regular competitor in MCC trials, winning several PAs in her Ford special 'The Dustbin' before making a name for herself in big-time international rallying.

DEREK JONES

Builder, comedian, ventriloquist, conjuror and compère by trade or inclination, Derek is best known to MCC members as Chief Official in the Land's End Trial, a job he treats with extreme professionalism. He is known, too, as a member of Equity, the Devon Magic Circle and the Exonian Magical Society, and is often to be seen on-stage before removing his make-up and setting forth to officiate on the *Land's End*.

On the Thursday before the 1970 *Land's End* he 'lost' a treasured wristwatch while setting-up the hill on which he was to serve as marshal – a hill with a deep watersplash at the foot. Enlisting the help of the Clerk of the Course, he returned to the hill on the Friday and carried out a meticulous search for his lost heirloom – eventually 'finding' it and withdrawing it from the river-bed still ticking and showing the correct time! Unaware of this bit of sleight-of-hand, the Clerk of the Course was duly impressed by the craftsmanship of the old-time watchmakers.

Derek began his marshalling for the Club on Darracott Hill during the 1950s, and continued serving on the hill until 1964 – except for 1963 when, on a 650cc Trophy Triumph he had his first and only ride in the trial, an experience he hopes to repeat. In 1965 he transferred his services to Sutcombe Hill in his home village, for the first visit to the hill by the Land's End Trial. As a member of the Sutcombe Parish Council, he is a valued ambassador for the MCC among the local people – who might otherwise object to the peace of their village being disturbed.

MAJOR R. I. MARIANS, OBE

One of the names that will for ever be associated with the MCC, Reggie joined the club in 1909. Though he had a very limited competition career, from the time he became Club Captain in 1939 he never missed an event in which he was either a Chief Official or Steward. He was also responsible for many social events, and for the organisation of every Continental Tour during the early post-World War II years. His first motor-cycle was a $1^1/_2$hp FN, back in 1908, which he changed for a P and M (made by his mother's family) and, with wicker sidecar attached, rode it in the 1911 Edinburgh Trial. This and a Brooklands High-Speed Trial in the twenties, were his only two events. He became President of the Club in 1974.

He was a full-time regular soldier, serving in the Royal Fusiliers, and was wounded early in World War I. In 1918 he was posted to GHQ Ireland as Assistant Adjutant General, and retired in 1933.

In 1939, after much haggling and pulling-of-strings, he was allowed to re-join the Army as a Training Officer, and ended his service in 1948 as President of Courts Marshal and Military Courts, Home Counties.

As Chief Official he will always be remembered for his smart, military attire – light fawn riding coat, dark brown 'pork-pie' hat, brand-new Official's arm-band, and his polite and friendly 'Good morning' greeting for *every* competitor.

J. A. ('JACKIE') MASTERS

'Happy days, happy memories' – Jackie's words seemed to sum him up, for he had his fill of both. Elected Secretary of the MCC in 1925, he held this position until his death 40 years later; and in 1930 he was elected Trials Organiser, applying himself brilliantly to this job for the next 35 years.

From his earliest years it was always 'Something on wheels', and while still in his teens he was among the prize-winners on the cycle-racing tracks at Crystal Palace, Wood Green and Putney. It was, however, the first London-to-Brighton Run in 1896 that ended his allegiance to the pedal- cycles for, by 1899, he was riding a De Dion tricycle. This was followed in quick succession by a front-drive Werner, $2^1/_4$hp Jehu, Kerry, Abingdon, Vindex, Triumph, Ariel and Royal Enfield. In 1904 he acquired a 3hp Rex and, in 1907, he progressed to a 5/6hp, twin-cylinder, two-speed model of the same make. Among his earliest sidecar outfits was a Montgomery Flexible, in effect a banking sidecar outfit with the sidecar attached to the machine by two flexible joints.

It was in 1908 that he first became associated with the MCC, when he rode his Rex in the Inter-Club Team Trial, representing the Finchley Conservative

Club. This association with, and service for, the MCC continued until his death, always seeking perfection, always pouring oil on troubled waters and always accompanied by his wife Bea. His association with Harley-Davidson began in 1914; in 1919, when this American company sent over four specially-built 7/9hp engines for use at Brooklands, Jackie installed one in his trials sidecar outfit. He was so enthralled by its performance that he fitted it into a lightweight frame for one of his staff, S. H. Davidson, to attack – and secure – various records, and to become the first man to exceed 100mph on a motor-cycle in this country. Jackie continued racing sidecar outfits until around 1923, when his managing director (with strong support from Bea) impressed upon him that his neck was of far greater value than the many cups he was accumulating.

From then on he devoted his entire attention to the MCC. Always at the finish of the *Exeter* and *Edinburgh*, and at the foot of Beggars' Roost in the *Land's End* – with his familiar checked tweed overcoat – he glowed with pleasure as the competitors passed through his hands. And always at his side was Bea, looking as if she had just come through a West End stage-door. The stories and humour that accompanied the gins-and-tonics afterwards kept the ever-changing audience amused for hours. Jackie and Bea seemed inseparable – even in the early days when they did a lot of tandem riding with the Portsmouth Road Cycle Club, and the methods of controlling a tandem from the front or rear seats were not always in unison after a lunchtime session at the 'Wisley Huts'.

With his great experience, Jackie was often asked to give a hand in the organisation of events outside the MCC. These included the Light Car Club's Brooklands three-hour relay race, and the SMM and T's Golden Jubilee celebrations which featured a parade of 472 cars around the West End of London. In post-World War II years, he was very well known and popular in the motor industry too, as Public Relations Officer of the Rootes Group.

JACK POUNCEY

A native of Wimbourne, Dorset, and now in his eighties, Jack is a horticultural judge, lecturer and writer. Having joined the MCC in 1926, he has habitually ridden what must be regarded as underpowered motor-cycles for such a hefty six-footer. Initially a Dunelt works rider, he turned to building his own Pouncey machines when his sponsors refused to develop their motor-cycles along the lines he advised. Though there was nothing revolutionary about the Pouncey, it handled well and, after working day and night with very little sleep, he completed the first three in time to enter them as a team in the 1930 Exeter Trial. In a somewhat different field, Jack also went into production

John, the younger of the two Tucker-Peake brothers, concentrates hard as he picks his way through a section on an early Vincent HRD – not the most suitable of trials bikes but one on which he scored some startling successes.

with pressed-steel dinghies!

Much later in life, when he was approaching eighty and still competing in trials with a sidecar outfit, he suffered from angina, for which some sort of tranquilizer tablets were prescribed to calm his old heart during the ascents of observed sections. Normally, it was straightforward enough; he consumed a pill in anticipation of an exciting section, and it took effect in time for the climb. Sadly, and unpredictably, there was a lengthy delay at one particular section while officials cleared the hill of 'failures'. By the time Jack's turn came, the soothing effects of his pill had worn off – and he suffered a heart attack on the way up! Had it not been for this near-disaster, Jack would no doubt still be storming the MCC hills on his sidecar outfit.

GEORGE F. SIMPSON

A leading member of the Edinburgh and District Motor Cycle Club, George was enlisted into the MCC in 1934 by Jackie Masters who hoped that his expertise in running the Scottish Six Days' Trial would help Jackie in organising the northern route and finish of the MCC's Edinburgh Trial – a section that had been seriously lacking in worthwhile observed sections. As a result, the *Edinburgh* grew considerably in stature, and George's efforts were recognised in 1948, when he was made an honorary member, and in 1952 when he was presented with an engraved tankard in honour of his services.

He is a life member of the Royal Scottish AC, the Edinburgh and District MCC, the AA, and the Scottish Austin Seven Club. Better known perhaps are his successful ascent and descent of Ben Nevis on 19 October 1928 in a standard Austin Seven tourer – an achievement that is included in *The Guinness Book of Records* under the heading 'Mountain Driving'. He took 7 hours 23 minutes to reach the summit, and the odometer recorded a distance of 8 miles; the 'official' distance is 5 miles, the difference being accounted for by wheelspin.

Ben Nevis had been climbed on two previous occasions – and since, in the 1960s by a Land-Rover in 8 hours 40 minutes; and a GNAT was virtually man-handled to the top in 9 hours 10 minutes. Another MCC member, the late Sydney Allard made an attempt with one of his Allard Special trials cars – but rolled over several times down the mountain-side and had a miraculous escape. As the track has since deteriorated so badly as to become almost un-negotiable, George Simpson's assault seems likely to stand as a record for all time.

THE TUCKER-PEAKES

The name Tucker-Peake (or derivatives of it, as daughters have married and

When John Tucker-Peake died the club erected this seat in his memory overlooking Darracott Hill where it can be enjoyed by MCC spectators and local walkers.

changed their names) crops up with almost monotonous regularity in MCC affairs since the late 1920s . . .John and brother H. W. ('Tucker'), and the latter's wife Bety and daughters Maralyn and Susan. Apprenticed to Sir Henry Birkin's Bentley workshops at Welwyn, Tucker moved on to the Vincent HRD factory, building motor-cycles, and then to ERA at Bourne, taking part in a variety of trials and speed events – at first on motor-cycles, sometimes with Bety herself as the entrant. So that both could compete in company, he moved to four wheels, making a name for himself in an MG Magnette special (modified to TT NE specification), and subsequently the Tucker-MG – the bodywork of each being extended to accommodate four, as the two daughters grew up.

Maralyn eventually took to trials herself with the 'Tucker Nipper', a converted Ford 5cwt van. With this special she had a very successful five years with sister Susan as passenger, becoming only the second woman ever to win the coveted Triple Award – and the first to win two. Upon her marriage in 1967, she and her husband gave up trials, becoming fully qualified, official timekeepers at big-time International races in Britain. Susan, after trying her hand at a few trials, took to saloon car racing – winning the 1976 British Ladies' Championship, which resulted in an invitation to join the official Skoda works team for a season's racing in Britain and on the Continent.

As well as winning a formidable number of trophies as a very successful trials driver, always with Bety at his side, Tucker was involved in organising sporting events of every sort since 1934, and with brother John was invited in 1954 to join the MCC Committee. Since then he has served in almost every capacity in the MCC hierarchy, as well as serving on the RAC Trials Committee; currently he is General Secretary of the club.

Brother John's trials career began in 1938 on a 250cc Villiers-engined James motor-cycle, when he was apprenticed to the Riley Company. After the war he advanced to the opposite end of the scale with a 1,000cc Vincent Rapide – which he demonstrated was not the unsuitable trials mount it seemed, scoring several outstanding successes with it. Taking to four wheels, he built and ran the famous 'Scarlet Runner' – a hybrid with contributions from several makes and models, with eight gear ratios, lightweight two-seater body, and 'fiddle brakes' operating separately on each rear wheel to help it round tight corners. This may well be the first appearance of a modification, now used on all out-and-out trials specials.

This was followed by the 'Olympic', less successful as a trials car but a splendid performer on the road. His third special, based on a Ford Popular with 1,600cc Cortina engine, was in direct contrast and would climb anything; it is still campaigned by his son Adrian. John launched the Club magazine *Triple*, becoming its first editor and producing it for eleven successive years.

A member of one of the greatest of 'MCC families', John died on 24 June 1985.

JOHN WALKER

Another who will be rememberd as an untiring and enthusiastic worker for the Club, Johnnie's first love was railways and locomotives. He was apprenticed to the North London Railway at the age of 16 and remained in railway engineering until World War II.

His first MCC event was the 1936 *Exeter*, when he drove a Singer 9 'Le Mans'. Between 1967 and 1984 he served as marshal in more than 500 events, and he was Competition Secretary from 1975.

THE WOODALLS

Both Victor and Bert have been MCC members and strong supporters for a great many years – Bert's wife Maggie since the 1950s, and son Simon an active supporter of the rear-engined fraternity as well as Secretary of the Classic Trials Championship.

Among the earliest to appreciate the potential of Ford-based 'specials' in trials, Victor and Bert built their first in 1938, making the Roy Fedden Trial the occasion for its debut. Known as the Wolseley-Ford Special it was based on the notoriously whippy Wolseley Hornet chassis-frame, with Hornet rear axle and Morgan independent front suspension – the advantages of which must have been totally obscured by the lack of torsional rigidity in the chassis-frame! It was propelled by a Ford V8 engine, and clothed in a lightweight aluminium body-shell. After the Fedden, power was increased with a Centric supercharger – and straightaway it won the Vice President's Cup in the Kimber Trial and a Premier Award in the London-Exeter.

Their Mark II Ford Special emerged in 1951, making its debut in 1952 with a Triple Award for Bert – and providing Maggie with the honour of becoming the first woman driver to be awarded, in 1955, the coveted Triple. More recently this family of die-hards has taken to rear-engined Volkswagens and Hillman Imps, suitably modified for hill-storming.

CHAPTER 13

The 56th (1977) Land's End Trial

By Bill Boddy (reprinted by permission of Motor Sport)

As our reports of the MCC Exeter Trial seem to have been enjoyed, it was logical to cover the same Club's Land's End Trial at Easter. What better way than to compete in it, for which purpose a Hillman Imp was generously offered to Clive Richardson, who had 'cleaned' the *Exeter* with an Autofarm Porsche 911. When domestic considerations prevented him form complying I readily accepted; it occurred to me that if I made a 'rounders' of it on every observed-section Clive would be pointed out as having failed, because his name was in the programme. Compensation, if you like, for his tongue-in-cheek remark that I was afraid to passenger him on the *Exeter* because of the terminal velocity of the Porsche. Which, of course, was nonsense . . . !

It did seem to me that an Imp might be more of a challenge than a Porsche for this type of event, especially one on non-grip tyres. I had happy recollections of the normal Imp and its variants, although I hadn't driven one for years. In Wales this is now a popular car, the old A35s and Morris Minors having been replaced by Imps; all the girls seem to have them!

Tom Lush was the obvious passenger on the *Land's End*, there being a happy link here, as I had met him 40 years ago to the day, when he took me to spectate on this trial in his 1926 Austin 7 Special; it ran a big-end during the night, I remember, but we came back to London on three cylinders and Tom then worked through the Sunday night removing the offending rod so that we could make Brooklands on the Bank Holiday, in this now 567cc motor car . . .

Driving to the London-start of the 1977 *Land's End* in the BMW, I was introduced to the Imp in which I was to have my baptism as a competitor in a modern trial only a short time before we were due away. It turned out to be a smart cream-and-blue car built by Chris Betson, who owns the Culverstone Service Station at Meopham. Its loan had been arranged by Norman Higgins of the MCC, an ex-motor-cyclist who builds Ibex trials-cars.

So here I was competing in the MCC Easter Trial, that splendid event dating back to 1908. It embraces a varied entry, a 392-mile route, some very tough and interesting hills, and fine scenery. Our number was 242. Reading David Thirlby's new Frazer Nash book, I see he gives this as the total entry in the 1932 *Land's End*; *The Autocar* makes it 254. The point I am making is that, in spite of rising costs, this MCC event is retaining its popularity, for this year's entry numbered 334, including the motor-cycles.

Breakfast over, there was a simple re-start test, in the car-park of The Frying Pan Cafe. I had not previously done an up-hill start in the Culverstone Imp, but, determined not to fail, I used plenty of those revs and all was well, although there was a strong aroma of hot clutch afterwards, the pedal-travel being short and the bite sudden. The first observed-section, Sug Lane, was a long hill. I thought the engine would poke its rods out as the Imp screamed up in bottom. We hit a cross-gulley an almighty thump, but surged forward again. The light steering gives very little directional control but somehow the right-angled bridge was negotiated and we continued to non-stop to the top. this gave me confidence, for clearly Betson's Imp knows about trials and was in its element on 13 inch Uniband Remould rear tyres. But those revs!

Dawn broke during the long road-section ahead, a mini-Grand Prix terminating for us when the n/s Uniband went flat. The ploy was to change the tyres round, so that we continued with Fisk Premier radials on the back wheels and a Dayton Mustang sharing the front with the surviving Uniband. These were run at 22 lb/sq in throughout, obviating the customary trials' chore of constant re-inflating. We had fun up Porlock (not observed) and descended Countisbury, to await our turn up the dreaded Beggars' Roost. Again revving unmercifully, we romped up, only to have the engine cut out a few yards from the main road, well clear of the section-ends notice. When the engine came up solid on the starter I was convinced I had dropped some part of the valve-gear. The BMW and Higgins' Vauxhall Firenza soon arrived, and Betson set to work. It was Higgins who removed the distributor cap to reveal an absent nut, which had deranged the ignition timing. I had also turned the fan-belt inside out (those revs!). It was a simple matter to cure these maladies and we were soon off towards the next observed-section, Orange, now even more optimistic. This muddy track proved no bother at all. We then followed Gray's Singer Le Mans along rolling main roads into the Devon lanes, to descend a horribly rocky wet track to Sutcombe. Amid the hiss of escaping air from other cars, as tyre pressures were lowered, we sat tight, and when its turn came the splendid Imp made easy meat of the winding hill and the re-start test, although for a moment, as I tried to save the engine, the revs dropped a shade and we hesitated momentarily.

It was then on to Darracott, another 'terror', set in wooded valley of primroses and tall trees. We were followed there by the courageous Sue Halkyard and girl-friend, in her Chummy Austin. There was an ominously long delay here.

When we were called up, the Imp was positioned astride the gulley at the start and got away well, to storm up the twisting steepness. I did not see the notice ending the first part and roared on up. Spectators shouting made me realise the mistake and as they said I could drop back to the start of Darracott 2, I did so. Lush was over the back, adding his weight to that of the light-alloy engine, but I kept more or less on the track and we then repeated the sure-fire demonstration the Imp had given on the first part of Darracott. The *Land's End* was taking its toll, however. Even at the start we had encountered the luckless Ladd with the sump off and the prop-shaft out of his MG J2 curing an oil leak onto the clutch. Later Way's Austin Ulster, on 4.00 × 19 Dunlop Trials Universal tyres, had broken a half-shaft and retired. Now, as we followed Sing's VW Beetle to the section, its spare wheel perched on its roof, Blackburn's Singer Le Mans looked to have its back axle in pieces.

The Imp was behaving marvellously. Before me there was a huge vertical oil-warning light, fortunately not glowing, oil-pressure remaining at 50-55 lb/sq in, and water heat at 60°C. A route-card error of some 10 miles made us worry about finding Crackington, but after we had turned back a lady who was waiting to see her son go by directed us and the right-hand turning and the left turn by a chapel duly showed up. Disaster lay ahead, alas. I took the little car safely through the water splash, which this year was deep, so that water came onto the floor. But when I came to do that surging take-off, the engine fluffed, and repeatedly dipping the clutch gave only a mediocre start. We cleared the long, steep, rocky section quite well and came to the very deep mud-ruts near the summit. I eased off as the wheels began to spin, Lush bounced, and we inched forward, urged on by the spectators . It seemed we might make it, but it was not to be. We stopped high up, so required only two pushes to get us going. Betson had run up behind the Imp, and he confirmed that its engine sounded flat. Water on something, perhaps? Which is all part of the MCC ploy! It was very disappointing, as I had hoped to do well for the honour of the remarkable little motor car. I had just got the feel of it on mud, too, remembering that there is no power below 3,000rpm.

Never mind! There was still fun to come. Barrats Mill, a long, rutted, muddy gradient, was a 1st-gear climb, amusing as there was no real directional control at the bends, the power at the tail-end, with a little drive-shaft 'doughnut' wind-up, and the Moto-Lita steering wheel trying to escape one's grip poking us anywhere (I believe these doughnuts gave trouble in the 1976 *Land's End*). Before we started this hill, Mrs Blight had reassured us that it was easy – her husband was at the top, no doubt thinking that his pvt Talbots would have made light work of it! A picturesque approach over a river bridge brought us to Ruses Mill and the double-re-start. We followed Keat's effective Hillman Avenger, and had no bother. Up the lane approaching Warleggan we spotted an early Albion Oil-Engine truck, obviously still in service – the hill was interesting but not a stopper and I was able to go into 2nd on the excellent Hillman gearbox. Next there was the Special Test at Galgeth Mount. Finding reverse gear elusive I let the Imp roll back over the reversing line, gunned it in sprint fashion to the finish, only to stop too early for the marshal's liking, thus losing a second or so moving over the line. No matter – speed was only a tie decider.

Finally, in the evening sunlight, we arrived at the sea, and Bluehills Mine. It is very steep, with alarming rocky outcrops. Chris had suggested I ease the Imp over these – 'Pity to break it on the last one'. I now felt I could control the urge and it was simple to go round the left-hand and right-hand hairpins of the new approach and gun it up the straight bit. The power, as the Imp pulled itself up the step on the inside of this second hairpin, was most impressive. There was no doubt that we would get up both sections of Bluehills. In fact, I stopped a little early before the re-start pad and the marshal said I could go forward, to a better spot. Off, and a flying finish, tempered by respect for the outcrops. I confess I did not see a stop sign, and continued non-stop to the Common.

Author's Note

I have closed this record of the long history of the Motor Cycling Club with Bill Boddy's personal story of a Land's End Trial in which he competed – for a particular reason. It is the only first-hand, 'I Was There' driver's description in the book; and it would perhaps equally well serve as a description of almost any Land's End Trial, before or since (with the make and model of cars suitably adjusted, of course). It will leave the reader with a feeling of the atmosphere that has existed for so long, and continues to exist, in these intensely popular events.

Though the annual race meeting at Silverstone is now for 'bikes only' (for reasons already explained), the three classic trials have continued through the years, changing only in detail – and *still* the entry lists are often over-subscribed. Among the competitors there are the hardy annuals, some now well advanced in years, who continue to compete year after year (still on two wheels, some of them) and there is the steady flow of younger newcomers, many of whom, one suspects, will still be filling-in their entry forms forty years on.

Maybe it is the 'touring' nature of the events that appeals, with the lovely places they visit – and the old, familiar observed sections which were tough enough to test the latest 'bikes and cars of the thirties and continue as potential stoppers for some of today's best. Maybe, too, it is because the events are suitable for everyday machinery – though, let it be said, well and circumspectly ridden or driven! Moreover there is something very special about events which, through the years, have attracted such names as William Morris, C. A. Vandervell, H. F. S. Morgan, Sammy Davis, George Abecassis, Malcolm Campbell, Kaye Don, Mort Morris-Goodall, Nancy Mitchell – and a host of others who were household names in the motor industry, and in international motor sport, in their time.

By no means least, though, are the lasting friendships formed – largely during the tense moments at the foot of successive observed sections as competitors await the time to address their vehicles to the steeply ascending, muddy, rocky horrors that lie in wait.

Appendices

Appendix 1
MCC Presidents

1901–1906:	S. F. Edge
1907–1908:	Major Sir H. E. Colville
1908–1922:	Charles Jarrott
1923–1924:	J. K. Starley
1925–1926:	Sir Harold Bowden, Bart
1927–1938:	J. van Hooydonk
1939	None
1940–1953:	L. A. Baddeley
1953–1954:	Sir Algernon Guinness, Bart
1955–1978:	Major R. I. Marians
1978–	B. G. P. de Mattos

Appendix 2
Brooklands Regulation Silencer

The exhaust pipe shall penetrate into a receiver to a distance of two inches. The capacity of the receiver shall not be less than six times the volume swept by the piston of one cylinder of the engine.

The top, bottom and ends of the receiver shall be straight lines and shall be parallel to one another. The ends shall not be at an angle of less than 45 degrees to the top and bottom lines of the receiver.

The exit pipe shall protrude into the receiver to a depth of two inches, and no part of this exit pipe shall be of greater cross-sectional area than the minimum area of the exhaust port of any one cylinder.

The pipes leading into and out of the receiver shall not be opposite to each other in the receiver, but shall be out of line to the extent of one and a half inches.

No device may be employed in the receiver which would tend to produce a straight-through flow of the exhaust gases between inlet and outlet pipes.

The exhaust gases must not pass direct from the exit pipe to the atmosphere, but must be finally emitted from what is commonly known as a 'fish tail' on the end of the exit pipe.

The length of the fish tail when fitted shall be measured from the end of the exit pipe to a point situated at the centre of the orifice, and the length of the fish tail shall be equal to the large dimension of the orifice. Thus, if the orifice of the fish tail is 9 inches by $\frac{1}{4}$ inch, the distance from the end of the exit pipe (where the tail commences) to the centre of the orifice shall be 9 inches.

The after half of the sides of the fish tail – that is to say the half of the fish tail nearest to the orifice – may be perforated with holes not greater than $\frac{3}{32}$in in diameter. The number of holes is not limited.

Appendix 3
Rear Admiral Sir Robert Keith Arbuthnot, KCB, MVO

On 31 May 1916, during the Battle of Jutland, the German light cruiser *Wiesbaden* was lying disabled after an engagement with the British battle-cruisers. Sir Robert Arbuthnot arrived on the scene with his heavy cruiser squadron, consisting of HM ships *Defence* (flagship), *Black Prince* and *Warrior*. They attacked *Wiesbaden* and were pounding her with gunfire when, out of the mist to the south, appeared Hipper's battle-cruisers and the German third battleship squadron. Both units joined the engagement and opened a withering fire on Arbuthnot's ships. Big fires were started in HMS *Defence* and, finally hit in her magazine, she blew up and sank, leaving only a cloud of black smoke to mark her passing. It is said that Sir Robert's Triumph, on which he had finished third in the 1908 Tourist Trophy, was on board *Defence* at the time.

Fellow motor-cyclists in the Royal Navy held Sir Robert in such esteem – not only for his many successes on two wheels but for his encouragement of clean, healthy sporting activities in the Service – that, in 1919, they inaugurated the Arbuthnot Trial in his memory. The principal trophy was a bronze figure of Sir Robert in contemporary motor-cycling gear. The event flourished at first, in the hands of the Royal Navy, subsequently being run by the Navy and Army jointly. Later still, in 1938, it was incorporated into the Services Trial, the Arbuthnot Trophy going to the best-placed Naval competitor.

After World War II, through lack of support, the event was dropped, the Arbuthnot Trophy going into safekeeping with the ACU. However, in 1980 the Arbuthnot Trial was revived by Ian Rennie and is currently run by the Salisbury MC and LCC in the selfsame area in Wiltshire that was used in

1928, when the motor-cycling journals were devoting three pages to their reports of the event. All motor-cycles must be at least thirty years old, British and with rigid frames; and the entry is limited to 150. A seventy-five-mile course is used, fifty-five miles of which are on muddy tracks and green lanes, divided into twelve sections and including two special tests of the sort used by the MCC, plus a timed hill-climb.

Appendix 4
Classification of Vehicles up to and Including Events Held During 1987

Motor-cycles fall into four classes—A (standard road tyres); B (pre-1965 British bikes); C (modern machines on trials tyres); and D (three-wheelers).

All seven of the car classes must use standard road tyres.

Class 1 is for front wheel drive cars.

Classes 2A and 2B are for normal rear wheel drive front engined saloons divided at 1300cc.

Classes 3 and 5 are for rear engined cars with a split at 925cc for Imp variants and 1300cc for the rest.

Class 4 is for normal two-seater sports cars with only limited modifications from standard.

Class 7 is for any car produced before 1941.

Classes 6A and 6B are for trials specials or production cars with extensive modifications and it is cars in these classes together with *Class 5* (mainly larger engined VW Beetles) which have to perform extra stops and restarts on certain hills.

MCC *Daily Express,* Redex and Hastings Rallies 1950-56

1950

General Classification : 1, MG TD Midget (S. Asbury), 4.008 marks lost. 2, Jaguar XK120 (Mr and Mrs Ian Appleyard), 4.015. 3, MG Saloon (L. Shaw and D. Lawton), 4.229.

Ladies' Awards : 1, Allard (Mrs E. Allard and Mrs E. Wood), 12.622. 2, Standard Vanguard (Mrs J. Cooke and Mrs B. W. Cooke), 13.093. 3, Sunbeam-Talbot (Miss S. Van Damm and Miss N. Van Damm), 13.578.

Team Award : No. 3 Team; MG Saloons (G. Grant and L. Shaw), MG TD Midget (G. Holt).

Starting Control Awards : *Plymouth* : Vauxhall (P. G. Weeks and M. R. Wiltshire), 4.861. *Norwich* : Singer (G. A. Duff and A. E. Adams), 5.115. *Harrogate* : Jaguar XK120 (Mr and Mrs Ian Appleyard), 4.015. *Cardiff* : Healey (A. S. Bassett and D. Hamilton), 12.829. *Glasgow* : HRG (W. Shepherd and I. MacLauchlan), 12.809. *Leamington Spa* : MG Saloon (L. Shaw and D. Lawton), 4.229. *London* : Morris Minor (H. J. Coombs and D. H. Laver), 5.078. *Manchester* : MG TD Midget (G. Holt and S. Asbury), 4.008.

Class Awards: *Up to 1,100cc (Open)*: HRG (J. H. King and M. D. King), 4.677. *(Closed)*: Morris Minor (H. J. Coombs and D. H. Laver), 5.078. *1,500cc (Open)*: MG TD Midget (G. Holt and S. Asbury), 4.008. *(Closed)*: MG Saloon (L. Shaw and D. Lawton), 4.229. *2,000cc (Open)*: Lea Francis

(B. B. Davies and J. C. Dixon), 4.422. *(Closed)*: Singer (G. A. Duff and A. E. Adams), 5.115. *3,000cc (Open)*: Riley (J. G. Searle and W. J. Searle), 12.686. *(Closed)*: Vauxhall (P. G. Weeks and M. R. Wiltshire), 4.861.

1951

General Classification: 1, MG TD Midget (R. A. Hopkinson and Mrs M. Hopkinson), 5.316 marks lost. 2, HRG (J. V. S. Brown and R. W. Kettel), 5.546. 3, Vanguard Special (K. Rawlings and L. J. Tracey), 5.586.

Ladies' Awards: 1, Ford, 1,172cc (Mrs J. Cooke and Mrs P. Copestake), 14.48. 2, HRG (Mrs N. Mitchell and Miss J. Bode), 14.998. 3, Sunbeam-Talbot (Miss S. Van Damm and Miss C. M. P. Hornby), 15.353.

Team Award: Vanguard Special (K. Rawlings and L. J. Tracey), HRG (J. V. S. Brown and R. W. Kettel), and HRG (G. A. Lewis and R. W. Ayres).

Newcomers' Award: MG TD (D. G. Griffin and A. G. Robbins), 5.677.

Starting Control Awards: *Plymouth*: Cooper-MG (J. G. Reece and P. B. Reece), 5.999. *Manchester*: MG TD Midget (R. A. Hopkinson and Mrs M. Hopkinson), 5.316. *Leamington Spa*: HRG (J. V. S. Brown and R. W. Kettel), 5.546. *Norwich*: Singer (A. Anderson-Wright and R. Baxendale), 6.438. *Cardiff*: MG (C. H. Davies and P. W. Price), 6.848. *Glasgow*: Healey-Elliott (G. S. Rollings and W. F. McCormick), 6,734. *London:* HRG (A. D. C. Gordon and B. Spencer), 6.03. *Harrogate*: Morgan 4/4 (D. Howard and B. S. Jepson), 6,279.

Class Awards: *Up to 1,100cc (Open)*: Singer (A. Anderson-Wright and R. Baxendale), 6.438 penalty marks. *Closed*: Morris (G. K. Le Grys and A. E. Westbrook), 14.693. *Up to 1,500cc (Open)*: MG TD (R. A. Hopkinson and Mrs Hopkinson), 5,316. *Closed*: Riley (G. F. Hayward and D. J. Scott), 6.671. *Up to 2,000cc (Open)*: Aston Martin (G. L. Corlett and R. G. S. Nairn), 15.116. *Closed*: Lanchester (C. Corbishley and H. V. Corbishley). *Up to 3,000cc (Open)*: Morgan Plus Four (W. A. G. Goodall and A. T. Hall), 6.126. *Closed*: Ford Zephyr (J. R. Smith and M. N. Hughes), 6.160. *Over 3,000cc (Open)*: Jaguar (F. P. Grounds and J. Hay), 14.278. *Closed*: Ford (P. W. S. White and L. A. Hunt), 14.328. *Special and supercharged cars, any capacity (Open)*: Vanguard Special (K. Rawlings and L. J. Tracey), 5.586. *Closed*: Sunbeam-Talbot (G. R. Hartwell and J. M. Sparrowe), 14.575.

1952

General Classification: 1, Dellow 1,172cc S (C. R. Hardman and Mrs M. Hardman), 4.76 marks lost. 2, Vanguard Special (K. Rawlings and L. J. Tracey), 4.80. 3, Morgan Plus Four (W. A. G. Goodall and A. T. Hall), 4.92.

Ladies' Awards: 1, Sunbeam-Talbot (Miss S. Van Damm and Mrs F. V. Clarke), 5.59. 2, Jaguar XK120 (Mrs L. D. Snow and Miss K. R. Whittelle), 6.52. 3, Rover (Miss H. N. Dunham and Mrs M. Blackburn), 6.82.

Team Award: MG TD Midget (R. A. Hopkinson and Mrs M. Hopkinson), MG (D. G. Scott and B. J. Warr), and Cooper-MG (G. Grant and F. C. Davis), 15.52 aggregate.

Starting Control Awards: *Plymouth*: Vauxhall (G. H. Turnbull). *Manchester*: Dellow S (C. R. Hardman). *Kenilworth*: Vanguard Special (K. Rawlings). *Norwich*: Fiat (A. C. Westwood). *Cardiff*: MG TD Midget (M. R. G. Llewellyn and R. H. White-Smith). *Glasgow*: Austin A40 (A. H. Senior and W. W. Metcalf). *London*: MG TD Midget (M. Wick and C. Wick). *Harrogate*: MG TD Midget (R. G. Godsmark and D. R. C. Blackhall).

Specials – supercharged, any capacity: (Open): 1, Dellow S (C. R. Hardman and Mrs M. Hardman). *(Closed)*: Morris Minor S (K. S. Chitty and A. J. M. Chitty).

Class Awards: Up to 1,100cc (Open): Fiat (A. C. Westwood and D. A. Corder), 5.65. *(Closed)*: Austin 800 (G. B. Flewitt and R. E. Lloyd), 5.71. *1,101 to 1,500cc (Open)*: MG TD Midget (J. H. Brooks and Mrs J. M. M. Brooks), 5.05. *(Closed)*: Hillman Minx (P. G. Cooper and B. Pybus), 5.40. *1,501 to 2,000cc (Open)*: Frazer Nash 1,971cc (H. Sutcliffe and Mrs P. E. Sutcliffe), 5.64. *(Closed)*: Bristol 401 (L. F. Parham and E. R. Parham), 6.06. *2,001 to 3,000cc (Open)*: Morgan Plus Four (W. A. G. Goodall and A. T. Hall), 4.92. *(Closed)*: Morgan (P. H. G. Morgan and Mrs J. D. Morgan), 4.93. *Over 3,000cc: (Open)*: Jaguar (D. O'M. Taylor and Mrs R. Taylor), 5.05. *(Closed)*: Jaguar (S. Moss and J. A. Cooper) 5.17.

1953

General Classification: 1, Sunbeam-Talbot (F. Downs and W. H. Bartley),

70.35 credit marks. 2, Morgan (R. K. N. Clarkson and C. C. Wells), 64.94. 3, Ford Zephyr (H. C. Roberts and Mrs I. H. Roberts), 60.09.

Ladies' Awards: 1, Morgan (Miss A. I. C. Neil and Miss C. M. S. Neil), 18.41 marks lost. 2, Jaguar XK120 (Miss A. Newton and Miss M. Newton), 24.30. 3, Ford Zephyr (Mrs N. Mitchell and Miss P. Faichney), 25.17.

Team Award: 1, Morgan (A. L. Yarranton and D. Thompson), 17.06 marks lost. 2, Morgan (B. E. Phipps and H. H. Priest), 16.42. 3, Morgan (H. Moore and J. M. Moore), 13.52.

Starting Control Awards: *Plymouth*: SunbeamTalbot (F. Downs and W. H. Bartley). *Manchester*: Bristol (L. S. Stross and E. G. Jackson). *Kenilworth*: Vanguard Special (K. Rawlings and L. J. Tracey). *Norwich*: MG 1,938cc (S. P. A. Freeman and L. C. Eversden). *London*: Riley 1,496cc (J. Williamson and D. C. Miller). *Cardiff*: Ford Popular (D. S. Edwards and W. Thomas). *Glasgow*: Austin A40 (A. H. Senior and R. M. Baxter). *Special Award for pre-September 1939 car*: MG (S. P. A. Freeman).

Specials and supercharged cars, any capacity: *(Open)*: Vanguard Special (K. Rawlings and L. J. Tracey). *(Closed)*: Sunbeam-Talbot (D. H. Perring and G. Griffiths).

Class Awards: Standard Production Cars (Open): Up to 1,100cc : Morris Minor (G. D. S. Perry and J. Ashford), 18.51 marks lost. *1,001 to 1,500cc*: MG TC Midget (M. D. King and J. H. King), 10.99. *1,501 to 2,600cc*: Morgan (B. E. Phipps and H. H. Priest), 16.42. *Over 2,600cc*: Austin A90 Atlantic (J. A. Walker and R. F. Twynham), 29.20. *(Closed)*: *Up to 1,100cc*: Wolseley (K. G. M. Pointing and Mrs A. P. Pointing), 15.23. *1,101 to 1,500cc*: Ford Popular (D. S. Edwards and W. Thomas), 11.00. *1,501 to 2,600cc*: Standard Vanguard (P. W. S. White and I. A. Hunt), 11.48. *Over 2,600cc*: Jaguar Mk VII (Major J. E. Osborne and Flt-Lt D. Brown), 15.78.

Modified Production Cars (Open): Up to 1,100cc: Morris Minor (A. H. McGrady and W. G. Logan), 13.38. *1,101 to 1,550cc*: MG TD Midget (J. H. H. Fisher and J. Reynolds), 16.33. *1,551 to 2,600cc*: Morgan (J. H. Ray and J. C. Dixon), 13.68. *Over 2,600cc*: Austin-Healey (F. G. Davis and Mrs V. Davis), 12.01. *(Closed)*: *Up to 1,100cc*: Morris Minor (A. E. Westbrook and G. K. Le Grys), 15.61. *1,101 to 1,550cc*: Austin A40 (A. H. Senior and

R. M. Baxter), 12.23. *1,551 to 2,600cc*: Sunbeam-Talbot (F. Downs and W. H. Bartley), 14.64. *Over 2,600cc*: Jaguar (J. Hally and Mrs E. P. Hally), 12.31.

1954

General Classification: 1, Jaguar Mk. VII (E. R. Parsons and Mrs J. G. M. Vann), 13.33 penalty marks (2.42 above class average). 2, Morgan (A. L. Yarranton and D. Thompson), 10.27 (2.00). 3, Triumph TR2 (P. G. Cooper and Sir C. Kimber, Bart), 10.46 (1.81).

Ladies' Award: Ford Anglia (Mrs Y. B. Jackson and Miss P. Faichney), 18.95.

Team Award: 1, Ford Anglias (Edwards, Baker, Anton), 53.39 aggregate. 2, Morgans (Morgan, Goodall, Yarranton), 31.77. Ford Anglia, Consul and Zephyr (Reed, Gibbs, Thomas), 76.05.

Starting Control Awards: Manchester: MG (A. Williams and G. W. E. Knowles), 11.36. *Glasgow:* Hillman Minx (J. R. Robinson and F. B. Baxter), 13.06. *Norwich:* Austin-Healey (H. D. Wise and H. D. McKay), 27.55. *Cardiff:* Sunbeam-Talbot (R. Davis and G. W. Best), 12.65. *Plymouth:* Triumph TR2 (P. G. Cooper and Sir C. Kimber), 10.46. *Kenilworth:* Morgan (A. L. Yarranton and D. Thompson), 10.27. *London:* Morgan (P. W. S. White and G. W. D. Vaughan), 10.86.

Specials and supercharged cars, any capacity (Open and Closed): 1, Triumph TR2 (R. B. James and J. C. Winby), 11.10. 2, Ford Anglia (A. M. Reed and C. L. Davies), 12.87. 3, Ford 2,262cc (A. Lineker and N. Shepperson), 14.63.

Class Awards: Touring Cars: Up to 1,100cc (Open and Closed): Renault (M. Hinde and R. E. Ball), 12.51. *Up to 1,300cc (Open):* 1, Austin (R. D. Paine and H. F. Vyvyan-Robinson), 12.89. *(Closed):* 1, Ford 1,172cc (B. J. Warr and J. D. Irlam), 12.32. *Up to 2,600cc (Closed):* Ford (W. J. H. Snellgrove and P. H. Brown), 12.65. *Over 2,600cc (Open):* Alvis (D. E. Lawrence and J. S. Turner), 36.82. *Closed:* Austin (G. H. F. Parkes and G. W. Howarth), 18.17.

Sports Cars: Up to 1,000cc (Open and Closed): DKW (J. W. S. Utley and Mrs Utley), 43.50. *Up to 1,300cc (Open):* MG TD Midget (A. Williams and

G. W. E. Knowles), 11.36. *Up to 2,600cc (Open)*: Morgan (W. A. G. Goodall and T. Hall), 10.67. *Closed*: Morgan (P. H. G. Morgan and Mrs J. D. Morgan), 10.83. *Over 2,600cc (Open)*: Jaguar (E. J. Haddon and C. H. Vivian), 11.15. *Closed*: Jaguar (L. S. Stross and Mrs I. Stross), 26.39.

Pre-war Car Award: Frazer Nash 1,991cc (R. A. Watkinson and D. B. Watkinson), 94.96.

MCC Members' Award: Morgan (A. L. Yarranton and D. Thompson), 10.27.

1955

General Classification: 1. MG TA Midget (S. P. A. Freeman), 15.73 marks lost (21.59 above class average). 2. Sunbeam-Talbot (A. C. Whatmough), 15.20 (8.75). 3. Hillman (J. R. Robinson), 16.10 (7.85).

Ladies' Award: Morgan Plus Four (Miss A. Palfrey), 18.17 marks lost.

Team Awards: Production Touring Cars: Standard Vanguard (J. C. Harrison), Hillman 1,390cc (J. R. Robinson) and MG Magnette (G. V. Howe), 52.42 aggregate. *Grand Touring and Modified Touring cars*: Ford Prefect (I. F. Walker), Ford 1,172cc (P. Bolton) and Ford Anglia (J. M. Uren), 63.87. *Production Sports Cars*: MG TF Midget (G. K. Hale), MG TF Midget (C. Shove) and MG TF Midget (S. G. Cobban), 55.98.

Starting Control Awards: London: MG TF Midget (I. Mantle), 14.35. *Kenilworth*: Morgan (A. L. Yarranton), 13.46. *Taunton*: Morgan Plus Four (J. T. Spare), 13.35. *Cardiff*: Austin-Healey (A. E. Westbrook), 17.16. *Norwich*: MG TA (S. P. A. Freeman), 15.73. *Glasgow*: Hillman (J. R. Robinson), 16.10. *Manchester*: Triumph TR2 (H. B. Jacoby), 14.20.

Ladies' Starting Control Awards: London: Aston Martin DB2-4 (Miss P. Burt), 25.79. *Kenilworth*: Morgan Plus Four (Miss A. Palfrey), 18.17. *Taunton*: No finishers. *Cardiff*: No entrants. *Norwich*: Sunbeam-Talbot (Miss P. A. Ozanne), 32.80. *Glasgow*: No starters. *Manchester*: DKW 896 (Mrs A. Hall), 24.97.

Class Awards: Production Touring cars: Up to 1,100cc: Standard 948cc (P. G. Cooper), 15.23 marks lost. *1,001 to 1,300cc*: Ford Anglia (J. P. Blackmore),

16.79. *1,301 to 2,600cc*: Sunbeam-Talbot (P. H. Browne), 16.49. *Over 2,600cc*: Jaguar Mk VII (R. B. Cade), 18.77.

Grand Touring and Modified Touring cars: Up to 1,100cc: Renault 748cc (S. D. Silverthorne), 15.33. *1,001 to 1,300cc*: Ford Prefect (I. F. Walker), 16.09. *1,301 to 2,600cc*: Porsche (E. J. K. Patten), 15.82. *Over 2,600cc*: Jaguar (G. H. F. Parkes), 15.98.

Competitor losing least number of penalty marks: Morgan Plus Four (J. T. Spare), 13.35. Also winner of *MCC Members' Award*.

1956

General Classification: 1, Triumph TR2 (R. W. Dalglish), 11.08 marks lost. 2, MG 1,489cc (R. N. Richards), 12.34. 3, Triumph TR2 (D. O'M. Taylor), 12.54.

Ladies' Award: MG 1,489cc (Miss Pat Moss), 18.60.

Performance on formula basis: 1, Ford 1,172cc (P. Simister), 124.84 marks gained. 2, Ford 1,172cc (Mrs A. Hall), 115.28. 3, Hillman 1,390cc (J. H. Robinson), 49.28.

Team Awards: Production Touring cars: Renault (S. D. Silverthorne), MG 1,489cc (P. C. Wadham) and MG 1,489cc (C. J. Plummer), 44.32 aggregate. *Grand Touring and Modified Touring cars*: No entrants. *Production Sports cars*: Morgan 1,172cc (P. H. G. Morgan), Morgan 1,991cc (W. A. G. Goodall) and Morgan 1,991cc (A. L. Yarranton), 58.14.

Starting Control Awards: Manchester: Ford 1,172cc (J. D. Irlam), 13.32. *Kenilworth*: Triumph TR2 (D. O'M. Taylor), 12.54. *London*: MG 1,489cc (R. N. Richards), 12.34. *Bathpool*: MG 1,489cc (J. M. Noble), 25.84. *Norwich*: Ford 1,172cc (D. J. Morley), 233.36. *Cardiff*: MG 1,489cc (J. N. M. Hills), 15.48. *Glasgow*: Triumph TR2 (R. W. Dalglish), 11.08.

Class Awards: Production Touring cars: Up to 1,000cc: Renault 848cc (S. D. Silverthorne;, 13.82 marks lost. *1,001 to 1,300cc*: Ford 1,172cc (F. E. Still), 157.30. *1,301 to 2,600cc*: MG 1,489cc (P. C. Wadham), 13.78. *Over 2,600cc*: Jaguar (R. W. Russell), 17.68.

Grand Touring and Modified Touring cars: Up to 1,000cc: Austin 950cc (D. R. Milton), 13.78. *1,001 to 1,300cc*: Ford 1,172cc (I. F. Walker), 12.96. *1,301 to 2,600cc*: Triumph TR2 (D. H. Wilson-Spratt), 13.40. *Over 2,600cc*: Jaguar (W. H. Morgan), 16.98.

Production Sports cars: Up to 1,300cc: Morgan 1,172cc (P. H. G. Morgan), 15.14. *1,301 to 2,600cc*: Triumph TR2 (H. B. Jacoby) and MG 1,489cc (F. A. Freeman), 14.70 (tie). *Over 2,600cc*: Austin-Healey (H. S. Ludeke), 426.98.

MCC Members' Award: Triumph TR2 (D. O'M. Taylor), 12.54.

Appendix 6
Trials Hills

Through the years, successive organisers of the MCC classic trials have scoured the Westcountry for observed sections, the steadily improving performance of the motor-cycles and cars being met by hills of increasing severity. Some of them have been used briefly, then abandoned as too easy (or too difficult); others have subsequently been metalled and put into regular use by local people. A few have maintained their role as 'stoppers', either in their original form or when 'doctored' by local enthusiasts – or by the MCC themselves. Almost all of them have become household names in the history of MCC classic trials. Those used in the *Land's End* and *Exeter*, being the best known both to spectators and competitors, are listed here.

LAND'S END TRIAL

Barton Steep, Somerset: Approximately 1 mile from Beggars' Roost, left after Hillsford Bridge. Mild gradient, not rough, and used for special tests. Now tarred.

Beggars' Roost, Barbrook Mill: First used in 1922 *Land's End*; 900 yards long; maximum gradient 1 in 3.6; right-hand bend after 50 yards.

Bluehills Mine, Wheal Kitty, near St Agnes: Originally very sharp left-hand hairpin, 1 in 3½ on inside; rest of hill 1 in 5, ½-mile long. Hill abandoned in 1936 when surrounding moorland was rented by MCC, and today's hill was developed in two stages (1936 and 1937) from a disused miners' track.

Cloutsham, Somerset, near Luccombe: Private property. Used once for solo motor-cycles in 1931; 300 yards long, 1 in 4. Moderate approach, very sharp right-hand hairpin after which gradient stiffens and surface is a sea of rock. Track swings back to left, followed by series of rock steps and boulders.

Crackington, Cornwall (named Mineshop by other clubs): Relies on gradient and slippery surface after two water-splashes (one was led through a pipe in 1959). Used as test hill up to 1939.

Crossleigh, Cornwall, near Stratton: Turns right and left on loose stones, mud and rock. Approximately 1 in 5. Nearly wrecked 1961 *Land's End* through inability of rescue vehicles to cope with failures!

Cutliffe Lane (alias Cunlif or Cunderley), N. Devon: Sharp right through gate on 1 in 5, stiffening to 1 in 2¾; loose surface, 75 yards long; approached through private property. First inspected by MCC in 1938 and first used in 1965.

Darracott, North Devon: County boundary at stream at foot of hill. Misnamed Gooseham by other clubs – and so called for its first *Land's End* in 1933; 400 yards long, two left and one right bends, maximum 1 in 4. Used to be a timed climb in NW London Team Trial and in *Land's End* had a stop-and-restart test on steep first part.

Doverhay, Somerset: First *Land's End* in 1932. Rises to left from Porlock village; take right fork by garage. Long, steep section rising to 1 in 3½ at sharp right hairpin and immediately left. Surface loose but good even when wet. Used only for motor-cycle classes in *Land's End* – but also for cars in the short Devon trials.

Edbrooke, Somerset: Off to right of Winsford-Coppleham cross-road. Starts on fair gradient, with right and left bends at steepest, 1 in 4 section. Good, hard stone surface; easy when dry.

Grabhurst, Timberscombe, Somerset: Turn by filling station and in 500 yards turn right. Long climb to left and right S-bend; 1,000 yards long, maximum 1 in 5½, loose shale with very rough descent on other side. Last used in 1957.

Grass Park, Charles, near South Molton: Used only in 1931 *Land's End.* Loose stony surface with 1 in 5 approach to left bend; 250 yards long; steepens to 1 in 4 on right and left bends.

Hustyn, Cornwall: Steep, winding descent through Burlone Eglos to shallow water-splash. Originally hard stone surface; later very rough; ½-mile long, 1 in 4. First used for 1931 *Land's End;* now tarred.

Lynn Hill, Somerset: Turn off left on Lynmouth to Barnstaple road, 1 mile from Lynmouth at Cottage Inn. Very sharp left and right hairpins; 600 yards long, 1 in 4. Used in 1932, 1948, 1949 and 1950.

Marsland, corresponding hill to Trevail Bridge. Approximately ¼-mile long, easy 1 in 5 on leaf muld on hard surface.

New Mill, nr. Boscastle, Cornwall: Approach through ford, steep right-hand and very sharp left-hand hairpins. Good surface. First used 1938; last used 1961.

Oldrey, Somerset: Very rough after start, through gate to left bend; not difficult though might be when wet. Used only in 1957.

Orange, nr. Taddiport, Devon: Gradient 1 in 5, 200 yards long, slippery when wet. First used 1963.

Old Stoney, West Cornwall: Known to have been used once – probably before 1931. Surface good as inspected in 1969, stone-covered, narrow – and would need to be wet to be competitive. Now scheduled as bridleway.

Porlock, Somerset (A39): First successful car ascent by S. F. Edge in 1900, driving 4-cylinder Napier – for a wager of £50. First used by MCC in 1920. Rises 1,200 feet, 2½ miles long, gradient 1 in 4 with right and left hairpins. Now tarred and in daily use.

Ruses Mill, Cornwall: Starts between buildings, with right-angled turn, then two left- and one right-hand hairpins; surface mostly hard shale when used in 1930, 1931 and 1932, slippery when wet. Tarred since World War II; used in 1976.

Station Lane, Lynton: Rises straight out of town; loose surface; ¼-mile long, 1 in 4. Partly tarred since World War II. First used in 1933, last used 1965.

Southern Wood, Somerset: Two sections; north side fairly steep, loose surface; right bend near top. South side much steeper, mainly dirt surface, very bad when wet. Used in 1961 but cut out after heavy rain.

Stoney Street, Somerset: Luccombe to Webbers Post; leads off village with long climb past cottages; bad drop on left. At top, steep and loose bends on 1 in 4½ gradient.

Sutcombe, Devon: At village of same name, rough lane leads through water-splash. On west side straight and very rough; on east side, surface good with left-hand bend. Liable to be damp and slippery.

Trevail, north Devon: Runs up same valley as Darracott. Starts in water-splash with deep mud. Climbs slippery track, not rough, with three hairpins. Maximum gradient about 1 in 4½; ½-mile long. Used in 1965.

Treworgie, North Cornwall: Approach down rough track to brook; winds up through wood on all-mud surface and through farmyard.

Yeascombe (Exford), near Welland: Proceed as for Exford along north bank of River Exe for ¾-mile. Sharp left through river; good surface, steepens to rock outcrop; maximum gradient 1 in 3½; 700 yards long.

EXETER TRIAL

It was not until the 1930s that the trial went west of Exeter; until then, Peak, White Sheet and Black Hill were included. Subsequently, among the better known hills to be included were Meerhay, Devenish Pitt, Higher Rill,

Ibberton Church and Marlpits. Shortened trials, starting and finishing at Exeter in 1949 and 1950, included the less known Coombe Kennel and The Retreat – both east of the A38 and A380 in the Gappah, Ideford and Coombe districts.

Cucknowle, Dorset: Near Corfe Castle; forks left off road up over hillside, open for 100 yards. Bends left on steepest part (1 in 4); rough and rutted. Used for stop-and-restart. Road fenced off by 1964.

Devenish Pitt, near Farway, Devon: Left at farm; loose and rutted with maximum gradient 1 in 4½; ½-mile long. Last used 1931. Long since tarred.

Farwell, Devon: South of Streetes and up same hillside; good stone surface overlaid with grass; easy night hill in 1965.

Fingle Bridge, Devon: Near Drewsteignton. After 100 yards, right-hand hairpin on 1 in 5; average gradient 1 in 5 through nine hairpins; shale and loose stones, 1 mile long. First used in 1932; 81 failed. In 1933, 99 failed.

Harcombe, Devon: 1 mile from Sidbury; four sharpish bends at summit where gradient is 1 in 4½. Now tarred.

Higher Rill, Devon: In use in 1931 for stop-and-restart (9 failed). Approaches too bad for 1965 event.

Ibberton Church Hill (The Halter Path): Turn right 1 mile from Sturminster Newton or Blandford road to Okeford Fitzpaine, where fork right; sharp left and right turns at bottom; ½-mile long, 1 in 4½. Now graded footpath. Last used 1934.

Knowle Lane, Dorset: Near Loders; a mild hill first used in 1937. Starts at right-angles to metalled road. Narrow and rutted between high banks. Deep ruts and very rough by 1965.

Marlpits, Devon: Near Honiton on road to Roncombe Gate. Acute left bend at top. Maximum gradient 1 in 5½; ¾-mile long.

Meerhay, Dorset: Near Beaminster; very rocky surface with rock outcrops; 1 in 4½ at steepest, generally 1 in 5½; ¾-mile long. First used 1929.

Pin Hill, Devon: Approached along narrow lane to wide climb with S-bend; good surface, later tarred. First used 1937.

Rosbury, Devon: Off Crediton to Tedburn St Mary road. Longish hill approx 1 in 6; good stone under mud. Used 1965.

Ryall Hill, between Charmouth and Bridport: Used only in 1938, solos only. Very narrow, with sharp left bend.

Stonelands, Devon: Long stony track up through wood – inclined to be very rough and not often used. Partly scheduled, now, as a footpath. First inspected 1932.

Tillerton, Devon: Mile gradient, rutted mud. RAC Black Spot since 1961.

Waterloo, Dorset: Rises from Branscombe valley; right turn at start around farm; loose surface for 100 yards. Sharp right before gate; narrow with two sharp bends; gradient 1 in 4½.

Windout, Devon: Water-splash and steep, short approach to right bend, right hairpin on 1 in 3¾ and bend at top. Good but loose surface.

Woodhayes, near Axminster: Long muddy lane with little gradient. Used once, in 1938. Now overgrown and not useable.

Simms Hill, Devon: Slight left bend on 1 in 5, sharp right, then 60 yards on average gradient 1 in 3½; steepest 1 in 2¾; 200 yards long. New to *Exeter* in 1933; 18 climbed, 212 failed.

Streetes, Devon: On same ridge of hills as Higher Rill. Fairly steep, narrow, straight and rough. Always causes trouble as stop-and-restart.

West Sandford, Devon: NW of Crediton; 1 in 7, ¼-mile long; similar to Knowle Lane but good stone surface under mud. Used 1965.

Appendix 7
Regulations Valid since 1 February 1988

1988 (CLASSIC TRIALS)

Class 1: Front engine, front-wheel-drive production cars (except vehicles in Class 6).

Class 2: Production cars built prior to 1941.

Class 3: Front engine, rear-wheel-drive production saloons (except vehicles in Class 6).

Class 4: Rear engine, rear-wheel-drive production saloons up to and including 1,300cc.

Class 5: Front engine production sports cars (except vehicles in Classes 1 and 6).

Class 6: Rear engine production cars. Cars fitted with torque-biasing differentials as original or optional equipment.

Class 7: Production cars modified beyond permitted limits. Rear engine production cars fitted with torque-biasing differentials as original or optional equipment.

Front engine cars manufactured on a limited basis conforming to accepted specification and listed by the RACMSA (kitcars). These cars comply with either or both of the following:

(i) Have the rearmost part of the front seat cushion(s) forward of any part of the rear tyres.

(ii) Have a wheelbase of ninety inches or greater.

Class 8: Non-production cars (except vehicles in Classes 4, 6 and 7). Front engine cars manufactured on a limited basis (except those in Class 7) including those which:

(i) have the rearmost part of the front seat cushion(s) rearward of any part of the rear tyres and

(ii) have a wheelbase less than ninety inches.

Listed Cars

Copies of the agreed specification for each car listed are obtainable from the RAC Motor Sports Association.

Motor-cycles

Class A: Any solo on standard road tyres.

Class B: Pre-1965 solos of British manufacture, on which trials tyres are allowed.

Class C: Any other solo on trials tyres.

Class D: Sidecar outfits and three-wheelers on any tyres.

Acknowledgements

This is not the first attempt to record the long history of the MCC. There have been others, abandoned because of the seemingly insuperable task of assembling information, much of which was thought to be lacking. That this latest attempt has reached completion is owed to the fact that it has been a team effort, involving many people.

The Minutes of committee meetings (such as survive) have provided the skeleton of the story; and, most important, they have recorded the steadily changing official attitude to motor and motor-cycling sport and its effects upon MCC events. But there are lengthy gaps in these records and, to apply flesh to the bones, it has been necessary to enlist the help of the many older members whose ancient entry-lists, route-cards, results of events and memorabilia have proved invaluable. To these, far too numerous to mention individually, I am very grateful.

Much has been culled from announcements, notices and reports of events appearing in *The Light Car, Motor Sport, The Motor Cycle, Autosport* – and *The Autocar (Autocar* since 5 January 1962) with happy memories of events I covered or competed in myself during thirteen years as sports editor and before. The bulk of this information is the outcome of hours of research by Tom Threlfall, present editor of the MCC journal *Triple,* in bound volumes of these journals held by The National Motor Museum at Beaulieu, resulting in many dozens of photostatted pages. John Aley, today's Chairman of the MCC, lent a hand with this task; he also assembled and captioned the many illustrations.

H. W. Tucker-Peake, whose family has been closely involved with the Club through many years, both as officials and competitors, has provided much information and has allowed me to 'milk' several of his 'History' articles appearing in *Triple*; he has also written the chapter on MCC personalities, having known most of them personally, and the notes on the Trials Hills. And there are those who have provided the illustrations – Colin Missen, Bill Boddy of *Motor Sport*, Basil de Mattos, Dr Jake Alderton, the National Motor Museum, Jim Brymer and many others. I would also like to thank the Quadrant Picture Library for allowing me to reproduce the drawings and pen-and-ink sketches by the late Freddie Gordon Crosby, which were used originally to illustrate reports of MCC trials appearing in *The Autocar* between the wars; the proprietors of *Motor Sport* for the use of Bill Boddy's personal account of competing in the 1977 Land's End trial; and the publishers of 'Ixion's' *Motor Cycle Cavalcade* for information regarding the early days of the motor-cycle movement.

I am indebted to George Bruce's *Sea Battles of the Twentieth Century* (The Hamlyn Publishing Group, 1975) as the basis for the notes on Admiral Arbuthnot's action at Jutland.

All picture sources, where known, have been acknowledged with the captions but I would especially like to thank the many club members and friends who have produced photos and prints from their personal collections.

Peter Garnier
Newlyn

Index

Page numbers in italic denote illustrations.